HOW TO start

A Q PLACE

MARY SCHALLER

Published by Q Place

Cover design by Emily Gibbs

First printing, revised edition, January 2016

ISBN: 978-1-880266-58-8
Printed in the United States of America

Comments about Q Place

"I wish Q Place had been around when I was a seeker investigating spiritual issues! This is where the action is: a safe place of discussion and discovery, where open-minded people can pursue answers to satisfy their hearts and minds."

— **Lee Strobel**
Former atheist and author of *The Case for the Real Jesus*

"Q Place continues the small group Bible study ministry of Neighborhood Bible Studies (NBS), deepening and expanding outreach to adults untouched by the local church."

— **Kay Schell**
Retired co-founder of NBS and author of many NBS Bible discussion guides

"One reason why Jesus' style was effective is because he related to seekers authentically and sought to understand their questions from the inside out. Q Place offers just such a format: where seekers gather to discuss their spiritual journeys, asking questions in a safe place in which their questions are heard respectfully as they are encouraged to consider the One who can fulfill their deepest longings."

— **Rebecca Pippert**
Author of *A Heart for God* and *Out of the Salt Shaker*

"Curiosity about spirituality, God, and even religion is at a high level in our culture—but so is confusion about where to go to discuss real questions. That's why I'm so excited about Q Place! These groups provide safe settings for spiritual conversations, allowing open and honest inquiry in a spirit of respect, trust, and personal discovery."

— **Mark Mittelberg**
Author of *Choosing Your Faith* and co-author of *The Unexpected Adventure*

"Few people are aware of the transformational power of a small group of spiritually curious folks gathering for conversation with a prepared guide. Q Place will be a catalyst for local churches and caring Christians to 'get it,' and change the way we reach our searching friends so that the average individual can experience the adventure of evangelism and life change."

— **Russ Robinson**
Small group speaker and co-author of *Building a Church of Small Groups*

"Q Place is long overdue. Christians want to learn how to talk about Jesus in normal ways and spiritual explorers want to be listened to without an agenda. Q Place enables for this conversation to take place and when people like each other, the rules change. Hooray for Q Place!"

— **Jim Henderson**
Founder of Off the Map and author of *Jim and Casper Go to Church*

"Q Place offers the perfect venue for spiritual seekers to openly discuss their biggest questions about God. It's an ideal resource for anyone who wants a safe and caring community to honestly explore faith issues."

— **Vip Patel**
Founder and president of JesusCentral.com

"Q Place is one of the most exciting outreach tools available! It offers an opportunity for people to gather in small groups and safely explore spiritual matters together. In this engaging environment people can discover the real Jesus!"

— **Nancy Grisham, PhD**
Founder of Livin' Ignited, professor, and evangelism consultant

"It used to be, in the not-too-distant past, that spiritual explorers and seekers listened their way into faith. Today people are talking and observing their way into faith. This requires a community of people living out their faith while offering hospitality in the form of listening. Q Place is on the leading edge of God's loving response to this shift in culture."

— **Todd Hunter**
Former president of Alpha USA and author of *Christianity Beyond Belief*

"At a time when the word 'Christian' or 'evangelical' in the minds of many conjures up judgment, or the imposition of faith upon another, Q Place starts with keen respect for the one on a journey of faith. With full confidence that the journey ends with Christ, honored questions by the explorer can lead the person to discover who they have been longing for without knowing it."

— **Greg Ogden**
Author of *Transforming Discipleship* and *Discipleship Essentials*

"Q Place connects contemporary spiritual seekers to Scripture and an affirming conversational community. It is ideal both for the spiritually exploring, and for the everyday Christians who want to serve them and love them toward Jesus."

— **Dr. Rick Richardson**
Professor of Evangelism at Wheaton College (IL)
and author of *Reimagining Evangelism*

Contents

Foreword

We are therefore Christ's ambassadors, as though God were making his appeal through us.

– 2 Corinthians 5:20

Ever since I can remember, I've been passionate about reaching out to the spiritually unconvinced. I'm not exactly sure where that came from but early on, raised in a Christian home, I somehow realized that lost people really matter. And eventually, I discovered that nothing quite compares with the joy of cheering on seekers as they take steps in their spiritual journey toward Jesus.

And so I've devoted myself to cultivating genuine friendships and initiating authentic conversations in an attempt to convey the compelling message of the gospel. I've tried my best to figure out the most effective ways of presenting the truths of the Bible with boldness, clarity and urgency while, at the same time, offering unconditional acceptance.

That's why I couldn't be more enthusiastic about this book, *How to Start a Q Place*! In 2008, in an effort to remain true to its original ministry focus, Neighborhood Bible Studies took the bold step to ruthlessly evaluate its current evangelistic effectiveness and make adaptations and adjustments wherever needed. I'm thrilled to see this unwavering commitment to developing a relevant, cutting-edge approach to reaching out to people far from God with the gospel of Jesus Christ. And I'm honored to be affiliated with the ongoing mission of Q Place to equip Christians everywhere to facilitate life-changing discussions with spiritual seekers. This book summarizes the process of how to join them in this great adventure!

As you prayerfully read and study this guide, let your imagination run with the possibilities! Just imagine something like this: You walk over to your next-door neighbor's home and you are greeted warmly and invited inside. Within a little while, the doorbell rings several times and before you know it, a group of eleven or twelve have gathered in the living room for an hour-long, highly interactive and invigorating discussion—about spiritual matters! People are refreshingly open and honest about their own spiritual struggles and breakthroughs. They are eager to wrestle with comparing what they believe, both intellectually and emotionally, with what the Bible teaches and what others are sharing—and most of them are not even Christians!

Can you imagine such a scene? I hope so. I've been training Christians to launch and lead these types of informal, nonthreatening, ongoing discussions for spiritual seekers now for many years and I've seen God use this tailored approach for outreach in incredible ways. I cannot get over the impact these kinds of group interactions can make in the lives of non-Christians and how God uses this approach to reach people for Himself.

Imagine yourself forming your own group specifically designed for non-Christians. Imagine identifying an ideal setting, maybe in your church, your workplace, or your neighborhood, and inviting seekers to join you on a regular basis for a discussion about spiritual matters. Imagine exploring the gospel message together. When you gather together a small group filled with seekers, it's only a matter of time before you'll give them a chance to discuss it, understand it, and embrace it. Who knows, you just might experience life-changing encounters that you'll remember for the rest of your life. And when that happens— when you play a role in leading someone across the line of faith— two lives will be changed for all eternity. The one who received Christ—and yours—because you were there!

– Garry Poole, speaker and author of *Seeker Small Groups*

Introduction

A Simple Story

For many years I lived in a small community in northern California with friends I had grown to know and love through countless conversations on the sidelines of kids' soccer games, baseball games, field trips, coffees, parties, and PTA meetings. They were neighbors, educators, coaches, or parents of my three children's friends. Most of them were not Christians.

On many occasions I had invited several of them to attend my large church in our adjacent community. The church was known for its excellent sermons by a gifted preacher, great children's programs, and a talented worship team. And yet it held no appeal for those I invited. Most of them graciously smiled and declined my invitations to church. End of discussion.

Periodically, to my surprise, one of my invitations would be accepted. Each time, I was sure that once my friend came, he or she would become a regular attendee and would learn what it meant to be a Christian. The Sunday messages were so compelling that I thought a decision for following Jesus would be made within weeks or months after that first visit. Someone would give a testimony in our worship services that confirmed the typical scenario of coming to our church and meeting Jesus there. Unfortunately, that had not been the result with those I invited. Was I a failure, or were the odds against that happening in my secular community? My friends would come once or twice and never come back. Why? I wondered. When I asked them, they said that the sermons just didn't seem to address their particular questions about God, or they felt like an outsider, or it just didn't seem relevant to their lives. These people were busy. And they were not sure it was worth investing their time to attend a worship service every week when they weren't sure there was a God worth worshiping.

I couldn't give up that easily. I had grown to love these friends and wanted them to know the same life-giving power that I had found in my faith. Occasionally I'd have a spiritual conversation with my friends over coffee or lunch. However, these were few and far between. And it seemed it was much more important to me to talk about God than it was to them. I would be so excited when we had the one conversation of the year about God that I'd usually blow it with my overwhelming enthusiasm to "download" everything they should know about Christianity in one sitting.

In late 2001, I spoke to two of my Christian friends, Kristin and Judy, about the possibility of starting a discussion group for spiritual seekers in our community. We started praying about who to invite and when to start. I use the term "spiritual seeker" loosely. Most of the people we considered inviting would have told you at the time that they were not actively seeking anything spiritual. They were skeptics more than they were seekers. But God placed them on our hearts as potential participants in our big experiment to have ongoing spiritual conversations with our friends.

We invited thirty women to come to my house to check out the possibility of a spiritual discussion group, which we described as a nonthreatening place to have conversations about God. We suggested using the book *How Does Anyone Know God Exists?* written by Garry Poole. This is one of seven books in the *Tough Questions* discussion guide series that is designed specifically for skeptics and spiritual seekers.

So much has happened since that first day. Each person who came back in the subsequent weeks and years has been profoundly touched by this life-changing experience, including me. I believe that God guided us through our discussions about faith-related issues, and as a result each person's understanding of Him deepened. We came to genuinely love and respect one another as well. Many participants had not known what it meant to be a Christian, to admit that we are sinners who need a rescue plan. Some had thought they were Christians, but had never invited Jesus into a personal relationship, and they became true followers of His. Others, who had no background at all in Christianity, learned what it meant to be followers of Jesus and decided to become Christians as a result of our discussions and the love that they received from us. God had used this group process to bring people to Himself!

Clearly this idea was a success.

I believe that my failure to reach my friends through inviting them to church is a common story. In retrospect, I realize I had wanted to point my friends to church so that someone else could point them to Jesus Christ. Why? Because I didn't really know how to point them to Jesus without bringing them to church. I thought I had to tell them the right things about God and defend the Christian faith in order for them to believe in Him. I discovered through this experiment in my living room that asking good questions, listening, and when appropriate, sharing my story of what Jesus has done in my life create an effective bridge to connect with people who are distant from God and disinterested in the Bible. As a result, I became passionate about helping other Christians start groups that were similar to mine. In fact, I began to envision the possibility of supporting a large movement of small groups where people in an increasingly secular culture could find a relationship with Jesus Christ.

In 2008, I became the president of Q Place, an organization whose purpose has always been the same as the one I envisioned! This book is part of that purpose; it is designed to guide you through the process of launching a small group with spiritual seekers, a group that we call a Q Place—a place for questions.

The Q Place approach is built on a foundation of more than fifty years of experience and the premise that people learn best when they discover truth for themselves in a small group setting. In 1960, former InterVarsity staff members Marilyn Kunz and Catherine (Kay) Schell launched a ministry in Dobbs Ferry, New York, called Neighborhood Bible Studies (NBS), an outreach ministry primarily to spiritually hungry people, most of them well-educated but biblically illiterate. Some attended a church. Others did not. NBS group discussions were focused on the Bible: its facts, meaning, and application. Over five decades, forty different NBS guides covering two-thirds of the Bible were developed, helping people discover God's message for themselves. From the beginning, this inductive learning approach was focused on asking good questions and listening well in the context of a nonthreatening small group discussion.

Neighborhood Bible Studies' small group discussions were effective not only in the U.S., with NBS groups in all fifty states, but across the world, in at least ten different countries and with one or more guides published in twenty-five different languages. In these groups, a rough estimate of a million people encountered God Himself through His Word. Many of them discovered for themselves that they needed a Savior, put their trust in Jesus Christ, and then continued to grow in their relationship with Him through Bible study.

In the fall of 2008, the name Neighborhood Bible Studies was changed to Q Place. Here's why: In the early 1960s when NBS began, most people believed that the Bible was worth studying. They were willing to try a small group where they could figure out what to believe about God, humanity, Jesus, and the church through studying the Bible. However, general respect for the Bible has diminished. As a result, most people in the western world aren't immediately interested in finding out what the Bible says. Nonetheless, people still have a hunger for spiritual truth, and under the right conditions, they will be willing to talk about spiritual questions. Some will ask questions that seem impersonal at first: "Is the Bible a reliable source of spiritual truth?" or "How can you know God exists?" or "How could God allow so much suffering in the world?" A growing number of people, though, are asking spiritual questions that come directly from the struggles that they are facing, questions such as: "What is my purpose in life?" or "Does God care about what I'm going through?" or "How can I be a good mom?"

The new name, Q Place, reflects an approach that engages people where they are in their spiritual journey, with questions that they care about. In a group where exploring what you believe is a natural, non-threatening process, looking into the Bible can become more and more appealing.

Four Simple Stages to Start a Q Place

How do you start a Q Place? We would like to make it as easy as possible for ordinary Christians everywhere to launch an effective Q Place. The process of initiating a Q Place has four simple stages:

Stage 1: Preparation

Stage 2: Invitation

Stage 3: Trial Meeting

Stage 4: Growth

This book introduces the basic concepts of starting a Q Place, with one chapter for each of the first three stages and two chapters for Stage 4: Growth, since it is the longest stage of a Q Place.

There are three essential elements in any Q Place: inductive resources, time-tested guidelines, and trained facilitators who are prepared to initiate conversations about life, God, and the Bible.

Q Place's inductive resources enable skeptics and seekers to wrestle with basic questions about God and the claims of Christianity in a small group. When people begin investigating questions that key into their needs, reading short portions of Scripture becomes more appealing. Q Place offers Bible Conversation Cards as a nonthreatening way to help groups enter into discussions of the Bible. As groups grow open to exploring more of the Bible's message, Q Place's discussion guides provide rich, insightful questions that help people discover and apply what the Bible says.

Time-tested guidelines create an environment for transparent sharing and vibrant discussions. The guidelines encourage group ownership, sharing the question-asking responsibility, refraining from tangents, listening well to one another, discouraging any person (including initiators) from being the expert at the expense of self-discovery, and allowing the Bible to speak for itself. These guidelines will be discussed in Chapter 5 and are also listed in Appendix A on page 95.

Q Places start with trained facilitators—ideally three Christians who have prepared together to get a group started and keep it focused. We call those who launch and facilitate Q Places initiators. They are not leaders or teachers or experts. They don't have all the answers, but together they build a respectful, safe, and loving community where everyone in the group can make discoveries. Questions form the framework for discussion, with the foundational principle of letting the Bible speak for itself.

The Q Place approach can be developed into an effective outreach strategy for your church—a Q Place ministry. See Appendix D on page 98 to understand the five phases of launching a Q Place ministry.

A Simple Way to Get Started

With preparation, most Christians are capable of becoming Q Place initiators. This book is like a roadmap. Its purpose is to explain the Q Place approach, giving you practical tools and confidence and guiding you through the process of starting your own Q Place. Chapter 1 gives a basic explanation of Q Place concepts, and Chapters 2-6 cover all four stages in the process of starting a Q Place. In addition, there are appendices that provide the Q Place Guidelines and Core Values, a sample Bible Conversation Card, and How to Launch a Q Place Ministry.

A triad of initiators can walk through a chapter a week together, supporting, encouraging, and praying for one another as they learn and practice principles that will equip them to start a Q Place. A small group of Christians could also go through the book together, and then start multiple Q Places. In addition, Q Place offers Initiator Coaching for those who would like to have the guidance of someone who has experience as a Q Place initiator and can come alongside them in the process of starting a Q Place. *(See QPlace.com/resources/coaching for details.)*

As you prepare together, the format of your group time will be simple:

Pray to open your time.
Review the chapter, going over main topics.
Discuss questions at the end of the chapter.
Identify next steps that you will take.
Pray to close your time.

When you get together, always open in prayer. This is God's work and it's important to invite Him into the process. After this, briefly review the chapter (or if the group hasn't had a chance to read it ahead of time, read it out loud together).

Each chapter includes the following sections:

Key Scripture (Bible verses relevant to the topic)
The Main Idea (summary of the chapter)
Understand It (explanation of the principles)
Mary's Story (a personal example of each stage)
Discuss It (questions for discussion)
Next Steps (actions to move forward in starting a Q Place)

After you have a chance to comment on the chapter's content, go through the discussion questions (Discuss It section), starting with the icebreaker that is included as the first question. Allow time for everyone to share their thoughts.

When you have discussed the questions, review the section called Next Steps. Determine which next steps your group will take, and agree on what you need to do to prepare for the following week's discussion. Write prayer requests down in a journal or in this book, so you'll remember to pray for those needs. The prayer requests will enable you to know each other better and to support one another. Finally, close with prayer. One person can pray out loud, or the group can pray conversationally as several people pray aloud for the prayer requests.

Why start a Q Place? It's probably the closest parallel we have in the 21st-century church to making disciples the way Jesus did. He chose twelve ordinary people to be on a journey with Him to discover God's Kingdom and a way of life that was full of grace and truth. The early church followed His example in how they made disciples as well. Twenty-first-century small group guru Bill Donahue notes:

> Small groups were an integral part of the early church structure. They were small enough to allow individual members to minister to one another, use their spiritual gifts, and be discipled in the teachings of Christ. In addition, they were vibrant and life-giving communities where evangelism could take place as unchurched people watched a loving and compassionate community in action.[1]

Facilitating these small group communities called Q Places is an honor and a privilege for all followers of Jesus. Enjoy the journey! It will change you and will give life to all who participate!

Chapter 1

WHAT IS A Q PLACE?

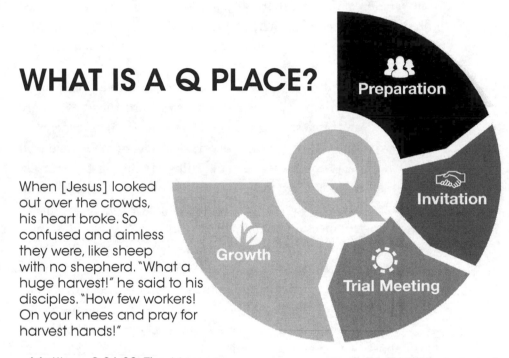

When [Jesus] looked out over the crowds, his heart broke. So confused and aimless they were, like sheep with no shepherd. "What a huge harvest!" he said to his disciples. "How few workers! On your knees and pray for harvest hands!"

– Matthew 9:36-38, *The Message*

The Main Idea

The primary goal of a Q Place is to give spiritually curious people a safe place to find God as He's revealed in the Bible through a facilitated small group process where the majority of the participants are not Christians.

Understand It

Jesus' heart was broken by His observation of the crowds around Him. He saw that they were confused and aimless, similar to sheep when there was no shepherd to guide and protect them. Like sheep, people wandered off, got into trouble, made bad choices, were attacked by predators, hurt one another, and didn't find what they needed to survive. There were so many in the crowds like that! He called it a huge harvest.

Jesus knew that people needed someone to guide and protect them. There were not enough workers to shepherd those who were lost, confused, and aimless. So He asked His followers to pray fervently for more workers. Who were the workers Jesus wanted? People who followed Jesus who could see the same thing He did: lost, confused, and aimless people looking for someone trustworthy to guide them. Jesus wanted His followers to love, guide, and care for these aimless people, having compassion on them like He did.

Has anything changed in the 21st century? There is still a huge harvest of people far from God and still very few workers willing to love them and build trusting relationships. The newspaper every day is filled with stories of people who are lost, confused, and aimless who have gotten into trouble. You personally know people like that. What would happen if there were enough workers in God's Kingdom who genuinely cared about people far from God and could serve as guides to Jesus, the ultimate Good Shepherd? You may be the answer to a "harvest worker" prayer as you listen and walk alongside someone who is wandering like a lost sheep and genuinely love that person through life's ups and downs.

While most churches today focus on attracting people to Sunday worship services, a growing number of people aren't interested in attending church on Sundays, listening to sermons, or praying a prayer to Jesus.

Yet, Jesus was clear about whom He came to reach. In Mark 2:16-17 (NLT), He was asked why He spent time with tax collectors and other known sinners or "such scum," as the Pharisees labeled many of the people Jesus attracted. These shunned people were clearly outside the established religious institution. Jesus said, ***"Healthy people don't*** *need a doctor—sick people do. I have come to call, not those who think they are righteous, but those who know they are sinners."* Time and again, Jesus modeled the principle of reaching out to people who didn't have a place in Jewish synagogues. He touched unclean lepers and healed them, cast out demons from people enslaved by them, and struck up conversations with outcasts, such as a Samaritan woman at a well.

In Jesus' earthly ministry, He gave ongoing attention to the twelve whom He had deliberately and prayerfully chosen. It's natural to assume that from the beginning they believed He was God. But the Gospels reveal that they did not. After Jesus' followers had been with Him for quite a while, witnessing many healings, miracles, and power over nature by calming a storm, **their hearts were hardened** (Mark 6:52).

Jesus surrounded Himself with a small group of people who were willing to be with Him. He spent time with them and informally discussed spiritual matters with them. He enabled these followers to discover answers about who He was at their own pace. You might say that this was the first Q Place.

What is a Q Place?

A Q Place is a group of two to twelve people who get together on a regular basis with one to three Christians (called initiators) to discuss spiritual topics about life, God, and the Bible. The Q is for questions, because questions are at the heart of every Q Place. Q Place participants are people who are willing to explore spiritual topics in an ongoing small group discussion. When a group is starting, it is important that a majority of the participants are not Christians. By being in the majority, they will feel it is safer to raise questions and discover for themselves what they believe, since they are all on a journey of exploration together.

The Q Place approach helps Christians go where people are, as Jesus did, and be the church among them. Like Jesus, a Q Place initiator enables participants to self-discover answers about God and the Bible. People can learn and accept new spiritual truths at their own pace as they experience a caring, nonjudgmental community.

What makes this approach doable?

Ordinary Christians can really do this, as long as three essential elements are in place: *time-tested guidelines, trained facilitators,* and *inductive resources.*

Time-tested Guidelines. People with diverse opinions about God can discuss their beliefs without serious conflict or arguments, but those discussions have to start with guidelines.

Q Place Guidelines help everyone come into the discussion as equals; no matter where each person starts, everyone has more to learn. When initiators pass out Q Place Guidelines cards and the group reads through them together, everyone can agree to the principles that set the tone for the group. From the outset everyone understands that they are there to wrestle with questions about God, the Bible, and what they believe, and discover answers for themselves. In the course of meeting together, it's simple to refer back to one of the guidelines on the card to help keep group discussions on track.

See Appendix A for the list of group guidelines. A Q Place Guidelines card is sent with every discussion guide order from Q Place.

Trained Facilitators. We use the term "initiator" for a Christian who learns how to facilitate respectful, safe, loving discussions, and then starts a Q Place—ideally with two other initiators. The most important aspect of initiator preparation is a close relationship with Jesus; to introduce Jesus to someone else, it's essential to know Him well yourself! Your close relationship with Jesus enables you to genuinely love people. Prayer and Scripture are essential for growth in that relationship. Spiritual friendships with others and a heart for serving are additional important traits.

With the essential foundation of a growing relationship with Jesus, a crucial aspect of initiator preparation is learning not to teach or become the expert in a group, but to facilitate and make discoveries along with everyone else, quietly communicating Q Place's four core values.

Q Place Core Values

Self-Discovery
People grow and learn best when they discover truth for themselves through discussion and study.

Safe Place
An ideal environment for spiritual growth is in a small group where personal dignity is valued and leadership is shared.

Spirit
God's Spirit will guide those who are spiritually open.

Scripture
The Bible and the life of Jesus are worth serious examination.

These core values provide common ground and create an inviting environment for the group. As participants continue to sense these values in the group you facilitate, they are likely to engage more and more fully, to take risks, and to experience God's work in their lives.

Q Place has many resources for training. This book is one of them! We have also filled our website Resources section with tools and equipping resources that are available through Q Place membership. Individuals may choose Free Resources to open many initial key resources, or Qplus to access the full range of resources for every stage of initiating a Q Place. One valuable Qplus resource is *The 9 Arts of Spiritual Conversations* curriculum, which helps you engage in simple practices that lead to meaningful everyday conversations about God with people who believe differently. Qplus also includes videos of a real-life Q Place getting started, an abundance of tools for healthy group dynamics, and an Initiator Forum for interaction with seasoned initiators and others on the journey.

Inductive Resources. Solid inductive resources are essential for dynamic discussions in a Q Place.

In traditional educational and religious institutions, a deductive learning approach tends to be more prevalent than an inductive approach. Learners are generally passive recipients of information—say in a lecture hall or a church. If there are study materials, they present a lot of content and are geared toward obtaining "right" answers to test understanding. With this kind of learning approach, you don't have to think much for yourself and discussion tends to shut down rather than ramp up.

An inductive learning approach allows you to be involved in what you learn, asking questions, making discoveries, and finding connections to your life. Thoughtful, challenging questions guide the process. Inductive materials create stimulating and diverse small group discussions through which people learn from one another with focused thinking about the topic. They help everyone in a group to make careful observations, well-founded interpretations, and meaningful applications to their lives as they discuss a topic or book together.

When participants have doubts or major questions about faith-related topics, an inductive approach provides ample opportunity to question, examine, discuss, and come to conclusions. Inductive resources open up the learning process so that participants can see for themselves and "own" what they learn.

Q Place offers a variety of inductive resources to fit the readiness and interest of all participants. Our website offers resources in the form of discussion guides, simple cards that may be handed out, a book of questions that can be passed around, and short video clips with questions that can be read from a screen. They cover topics about life, God, and the Bible.

From the beginning in a Q Place, initiators model a simple approach of asking good inductive questions so that the group can discuss them. As the group continues to meet, every participant can take a turn in asking discussion questions from an inductive discussion card or guide. This way, participants sense that the group belongs to everyone and they are all more engaged in the process of learning and applying what they learn.

So how do you start a Q Place?

There are four simple stages in the process:

Stage 1: Preparation. As presented earlier in this chapter, preparation starts with your own relationship with Jesus and a mindset of facilitating rather than teaching or telling. It also involves finding two Christians who will join you as an initiator triad, getting to know them, walking through this book together, practicing *The 9 Arts of Spiritual Conversations* as you build relationships with people who believe differently than you, praying for God to show you who He wants you to invite, and planning your invitations and your start date and arrangements for the first meeting.

Stage 2: Invitation. This is the shortest stage in the process, but it's a pivotal point! In Chapter 3 we will offer guidance for extending compelling invitations to "Come once and check it out."

Stage 3: Trial Meeting. This first meeting is all-important, and it's also fun! At the Trial Meeting, participants will receive their first impression of a Q Place and see if it is something that they would like to continue. Everyone will have a good taste of an ongoing Q Place when you as initiators have planned well and when you are carrying out your plan together. The plans will include refreshments, icebreaker questions, asking the main question, a short discussion of a small section of Scripture, and a time to discuss everyone's impressions and interest in meeting again. The main "God" question will help you as initiators to mention options for future discussions.

Stage 4: Growth. In the second meeting and beyond, the group will explore their questions about God and the Bible together. As everyone understands the guidelines for the group, you as initiators will model them in your interactions, cultivating an environment where it's safe to be transparent and to learn from each other.

There are three paths of discussion for future Q Place gatherings:

1. ***Discuss Life****:* Choose a life topic (such as marriage, parenting, pain, anxiety, identity, or life's purpose) that participants recognize as important to them at this time. Q Place Bible Conversation Cards offer short sections of Scripture related to each topic for the group to discuss using a simple set of inductive questions. *The Complete Book of Questions* is another low-key option. It's a book of icebreaker-type questions that are arranged in order of intensity and spiritual depth.

2. ***Discuss God****:* Choose a question about God that the participants identify as a key issue for them. They might question whether God exists, how He could allow suffering and evil, or whether He cares and involves Himself with people. To help initiators facilitate discussions around these questions without being experts, Q Place offers a discussion guide called *Tough Questions* as well as video resources produced by Explore God. In our Resources section, we have collected a number of Explore God's high-quality 3-10 minute videos with questions that spark conversation around these kinds of issues.

3. ***Discuss the Bible****:* Choose a book or small section of the Bible and use either a Bible Conversation Card or a Q Place Bible discussion guide with inductive questions to observe, interpret, and make applications.

Mary's Story

I had been a Christian for thirty-four years when I first considered starting a small group for spiritual skeptics and seekers. Even though I had become a Christian at age sixteen, for the subsequent fifteen years I had not taken my faith seriously. I didn't attend church regularly, read the Bible, spend time with other Christians, or pray regularly. I barely knew what it meant to be a follower of Jesus. Twenty-five years ago I was invited to join a small group. It was there that I learned through others and studying the Bible what it meant to be a Christian. I grew in my relationship with Jesus Christ. I started spending regular time in prayer. My everyday behavior and choices slowly began to change. As time went by, I was more loving toward others, joyful, peaceful, and kind. I wanted my friends and family to experience the same thing.

Eventually, I started to see those who were far from God the same way Jesus did: with a broken heart. By the time God started to "nudge" me to reach out to my neighbors and friends, I genuinely wanted them to know the source of my growing joy and peace.

Discuss It

1. *Icebreaker* (Choose one or more.):
   - Where are you from and what did you like most about living there?
   - Next to your job, what consumes most of your time?
   - What room in your house best reflects your personality?
   - What movie have you watched over and over again?

2. What made you decide to read *How to Start a Q Place?* What expectations do you have? What do you hope to learn?

3. Why do you think Jesus' heart broke when He saw the crowds "confused and aimless" (Matthew 9:36-38, *The Message*)?

4. Jesus said that there is a huge harvest, but few workers. Do you see yourself as a worker for the harvest? Among your own friends and acquaintances, who can you envision as part of that harvest?

5. Who else do you know who could be a fellow worker alongside you?

6. How does what you're learning compare with what you have been taught in the past related to helping people find Jesus or turn to God?

7. What are the four stages of starting a Q Place? Which one will be most challenging for you personally?

8. Imagine that you had never read the Bible, rarely had spiritual conversations, and had never been in a small group for discussing spiritual things. If a friend invited you to join a small group that was going to be talking about God, what would you need to know about this group before coming?

9. What do you think is the goal of a Q Place?

10. Why do you think guidelines would be important in a Q Place?

11. At this point, what value do you see in an inductive approach and inductive resources for discussing spiritual matters?

Next Steps

1. Read Chapter 2 and be prepared to participate in the next group discussion.

2. Go to the Resources tab at QPlace.com and check out the features of membership, including resources that will help you engage in meaningful conversations about God and prepare to start a Q Place. These resources will be referenced throughout *How to Start a Q Place*.

3. Think about which of your own friends and acquaintances might be interested in coming to a Q Place, and why they might come.

4. Spend time this week studying one or all of these Scripture passages. Ask God to use these verses to help you understand what He wants you to do regarding reaching out to those who don't know Him.
   - Matthew 9:35-38
   - Matthew 28:16-20
   - Luke 15:1-32
   - Luke 10:1-20
   - Mark 6:6-13

Chapter 2

PREPARATION

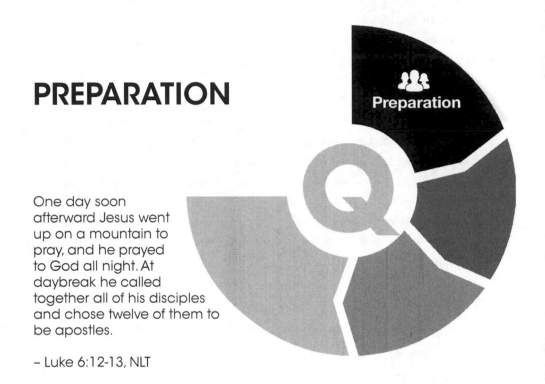

One day soon
afterward Jesus went
up on a mountain to
pray, and he prayed
to God all night. At
daybreak he called
together all of his disciples
and chose twelve of them to
be apostles.

– Luke 6:12-13, NLT

The Main Idea

The first stage of launching a Q Place is *Preparation*. Preparation involves four elements: preparing the state of your own heart and mind, finding two other people to initiate a Q Place with you, building relationships with non-Christians, and deciding on a time and location for your first meeting.

Understand It

The ministry example that Jesus gave us for making new disciples is one of relationship—of fervent prayer in relationship with the Father before choosing a small group of twelve, and then of three years' time in relationship with this group, pouring His time and energy into them. Through those years, Jesus lived life with them, engaged them in discussions, and challenged them to take action as well as to observe, think, and draw conclusions.

While Jesus prayerfully selected twelve individuals to follow Him closely, He invested even more of Himself in three men: Peter, James, and John. We have found that starting with a triad of three committed followers of Jesus is a powerful way to make disciples. It looks like this: three believers spending time in prayer together while drawing closer to Jesus; growing together in the Word of God; encouraging each other as they connect relationally with people they meet; and then selecting, inviting, and coming alongside several others on a journey in a small group community of discovery to come and see who Jesus is.

To launch a Q Place, these four main components are all part of preparation:

1. **You**, the initiator—the state of your own mind and heart

2. **Two others** who can partner with you (as an initiator triad)

3. **People to invite** who are spiritually curious

4. **A date and location** for the first gathering

You

It starts with you, the potential initiator. Do you have a heart for those who are far from God? If not, pray that God would give you that kind of heart. Let your heart be broken by what breaks God's heart: people who are living outside of a relationship with Him.

This entire process of starting and facilitating a Q Place will require attentive prayer with a genuine love for God and others. Jesus said He does only what the Father tells Him to do. Can you hear what the Father is telling you to do? In order for your efforts to bear fruit, listen prayerfully and follow God's leading. Since Jesus says that apart from

Him we can bear no fruit (John 15:4-5), our relationship with Jesus is a critical part of our ability to facilitate well.

There are three focused areas for attentive prayer:

- Pray that God would give you a heart for those far from God

- Pray that God would show you two other people to help you start a Q Place.

- Pray that God would show you friends who have questions about God.

Two others

As you are praying, be ready to move forward as God leads you, to invite two others to start a Q Place with you—as an *initiator triad*. King Solomon commented on the value and importance of not going into any kind of battle alone:

> *A person standing alone can be attacked and defeated, but two can stand back-to-back and conquer. Three are even better, for a triple-braided cord is not easily broken.*

> – Ecclesiastes 4:12, NLT

There is a spiritual enemy who will want to defeat and conquer you in your efforts to reach out to others who have not yet considered turning to God and the Bible. When there are three of you who are transparent and accountable to each other, praying and seeking God's direction together, the Spirit of God in each of you will guide your plans and your actions. Finding an initiator triad can't be rushed or solely our own idea. If God wants you to reach out to people around you, He will be the one to reveal the ones who will join you.

Jesus is our example. In everything He did through His earthly ministry, as well as through time and eternity, first and foremost Jesus was in a perfect relationship with the Father and the Holy Spirit. In the most perfect community ever, there are three persons, and each one is in constant fellowship with the other two. The Trinity—this "divine triad"—equally expresses the fullness of the attributes of God—His love, grace, truth, holiness, and power.

So, when Jesus led His followers, He wasn't acting independently, but in perfect communion with the Father and the Holy Spirit. If we follow His example in making disciples, we also will not set out alone, but with the community of a triad of believers, all in relationship with the Father, Son, and Holy Spirit.

When you start with three initiators, each of you will know some people to invite so that you will have a larger pool of participants to join your Q Place. Ideally those participants will outnumber you! Because Jesus is at the center of your relationship, the participants will not only experience a trusting relationship with you three, but they will also see Jesus in you! For more on triads, read *The 9 Arts of Spiritual Conversations* module 7.2, *The Art of Facilitating: How Can We Lead with Three?* (available digitally through Qplus membership or through the Q Place store).

People to invite

Along with praying for an initiator triad, pray that God would reveal those around you who have questions about God. Develop a list of people who might be spiritually open or curious. Pray through the list regularly, asking God to show you which ones He is choosing for you— to reveal His love and grace through you.

Building relationships is an important part of the Preparation stage, because the most likely people to accept an invitation to a Q Place are those who already know and trust you. Watch for where God is drawing you to start a Q Place. Is it your neighborhood? Your workplace? In your life is there a group of people who have a common interest, like golf, biking, or cooking? Or do you already have a group of mutual friends who are open to talking about spiritual topics if you make it safe to do so? God will give you a compassionate heart for those He wants you to invite.

As you get clearer on the group of people or the location, ask God to reveal a few Christians there who might initiate the group with you. Even when you haven't yet found co-initiators, go ahead and take op-portunities to meet and get to know potential participants for your Q Place. Every day you probably encounter dozens of people. Starting a friendship in an area you have identified may be as simple as making yourself available there.

Consider some of the following ways to make new friends:

- Make an effort to talk with people while riding in the elevator, working in the yard, taking a walk, etc.
- Welcome new neighbors with cookies or a simple meal.
- Join a sports team or take a fitness class to enlarge your circle of acquaintances.
- Coach a sports team or teach a class for the park district or community center.
- Host a game night or potluck for neighbors or newcomers in your community.
- Volunteer and build relationships at your child's school.
- Teach someone how to read through an ESL or literacy program.
- Volunteer at a food pantry, Big Brothers/Big Sisters, food co-op, recycling center, crisis pregnancy center, nursing home, etc.
- Join a book discussion group.
- Invite several friends or neighbors to work on a hobby or an interest you share, such as compiling scrapbooks, woodworking, or gardening.
- Accept others' invitations to go to an event or to spend time together.
- Ask someone to help you with something. Look for opportunities to return the favor.

In any of these suggested activities, follow the Holy Spirit's leading and ask people about their lives, their beliefs, and their stories. If you're spending time with people around you, learning about them, asking good questions, and listening to their opinions, you're actually getting grounded in the principles you'll need to facilitate a Q Place.

Again, our best model for building relationships is Jesus. If you look through the lens of the four Gospels, you'll learn common ways in which Jesus built trust among His followers. If you want to know the people around you, you will need to spend time with them to establish common ground; get to know their likes, dislikes, joys, and sorrows; share your life with them; and have authentic, caring relationships. They are not "projects." They are people who matter to God, just like you. Jesus hung out with His followers and knew them well. It took them a while to trust and believe Him. He was patient with the process of building relationships. It will take time for you to do that too.

When you develop new friendships, you can identify yourself as a Christian as God allows in a way that is transparent, appropriate, and vulnerable. Your motivation should simply be to give your friends a glimpse of what really matters most to you. There are two simple ways to do this. One would be to offer to pray for them if they share something with you that could use prayer. Another would be to mention activities or interests related to your faith.

While you allow your faith to come naturally into conversations with other people, also look for opportunities to find out what they believe. Ask questions that encourage them to talk about their lives. As they sense your genuine and uncritical interest, they will be more ready to trust your friendship and open up even more. In Ephesians 5:15-17, the Apostle Paul tells us:

> **Be very careful, then, how you live—not as unwise but as wise, making the most of every opportunity, because the days are evil. Therefore do not be foolish, but understand what the Lord's will is.**

Ask God to help you wisely discern opportunities that could lead to a spiritual discussion. Pray that He'll give you a significant question or comment at an appropriate moment. Then listen and understand your friend's perspective.

If you find that your network outside of Christian circles remains limited or that you're having difficulty building new relationships, you're not the only Christian to face that reality! It's such a common issue that Q Place has developed *The 9 Arts of Spiritual Conversations* (the 9 Arts), a whole curriculum series to help Christians engage with people who believe differently. You and your initiator triad may realize that your biggest need is to spend time cultivating relationships over time. You could decide to put this book on pause for a while in order to go through some of the 9 Arts modules together and practice them in your everyday life. In time, you are likely to find that starting a Q Place is a natural outflow of those everyday practices.

A date and location

When your triad has come into place and you are preparing together and building relationships with people you could invite, go ahead and set a date and location for the first gathering. It could be in one of your homes, but it could also be held in one of the participants' homes or in a neutral place such as a coffee shop. Choose a time and place that will be convenient to those you are inviting, and somewhere that is conducive to group discussions: quiet, with limited or no background noise, and free from interruptions like phones or other people. Even the seating should be considered. Arrange comfortable chairs in a circle, oval, or square.

Setting a tentative date for starting a Q Place gives you a good deadline to work toward your goal. If for some reason you aren't quite ready when the date is coming up, you can always move the date to another one that is more realistic. But you'll find that the planned starting date will often help your triad build momentum. The Preparation stage can sometimes take longer than you think. Be patient. God is doing a good work in you as He prepares to do a good work in those you invite!

Mary's Story

I knew lots of people in our town of Portola Valley through fourteen years of activities with our children in the local school district. In late 2001, I spoke to two of my Christian friends (Kristin and Judy) about the possibility of starting a spiritual discussion group for non-Christians in our community. I was willing to have it in my home. We started praying for whom to invite and when to start. Most of the people that we considered inviting would have told you at the time that they were not actively seeking God. They were skeptics more than they were spiritual seekers. But God placed them on our hearts as potential participants. I wrote down at least forty names and started praying for each person on the list every day. My prayer: Is this someone You want us to invite, Lord?

Discuss It

1. *Icebreaker:* Describe a time when you were well-prepared for an anticipated event, or when you were not well-prepared. How did the event turn out?

2. Who do you most long to come to know Jesus? Why?

3. On a scale of one to ten, what would you say is the "readiness" of your own heart to reach out and care for people who believe differently than you? Circle the number below that you think comes closest to your level of readiness and explain your answer.

1————2————3————4————5————6————7————8————9————10
Not ready   Ready

4. In your life, how has prayer affected the fruitfulness of your efforts to introduce people to Jesus? From now on, what simple steps can you take to invite God's activity into peoples' lives?

5. Why do you think Jesus had an inner circle of Peter, James, and John among His twelve apostles?

6. What benefits do you see in starting with a triad of facilitators before launching your Q Place? Challenges?

7. Are there people you already know who might be ready and interested in becoming co-initiators of a Q Place with you? What causes you to think they are ready? What excites you about partnering with them? If no one comes to mind, describe the kind of person you'd like to find.

8. Below or in a journal, start a list of people you already know who might be interested in participating in a Q Place. Describe what you have in common with them. (i.e., living in the same neighborhood or working at the same place). Start now to pray for them.

9. Of all of the ideas listed on page 33 for making new friends, which ones are the most natural and appealing for you?

10. What do you think would be the best location for your own Q Place? Why?

11. On a scale of one to five, with one representing a score of not being prepared, and five being well-prepared, rate the following four components of your readiness to start a Q Place:

____ Your own heart and mind

____ Two co-initiators to start a Q Place

____ Friends to invite

____ Location to have the first Q Place

Next Steps

1. Begin praying daily for the people you know who might be interested in coming to a Q Place. Ask God to show you which ones He wants you to invite. Are there names that God wants to add?

2. In conversations over the next week, practice asking questions that encourage your friends to tell you more about their lives.

3. Sign up for a Qplus membership at QPlace.com and watch the 15-minute video "Starting a Q Place: Preparation...The Triad." After logging in, you can find the video by typing "Video Triad" into the search bar.

4. Read and discuss these 9 Arts modules:
   - *The Art of Praying 2.1: Why Pray First?*
   - *The Art of Facilitating 7.1: Why Facilitate?*
   - *The Art of Facilitating 7.2: How Can We Lead with Three?*

   If you are a Qplus member, you may navigate to the Arts modules this way: After logging in, click on Resources Home (in the orange navigation bar). In the Resources menu panel on the left side of the screen, click 9 Arts of Spiritual Conversations and then 9 Arts, and then click on the art category. A list of posts will come up on the right side of the screen. Click on the 9 Arts module that you're looking for and the post will open. At the bottom of the post, click on "Download PDF" to access the full module.

5. Read Chapter 3 and be prepared to participate in the next group discussion.

Chapter 3

INVITATION

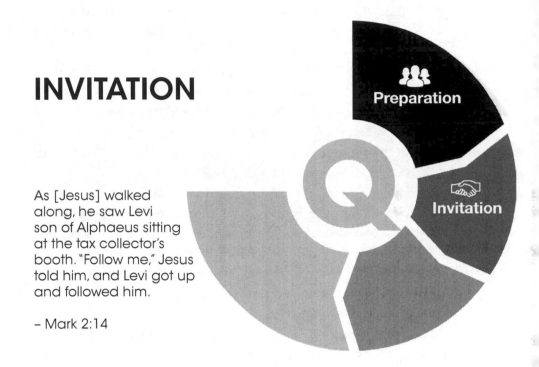

As [Jesus] walked
along, he saw Levi
son of Alphaeus sitting
at the tax collector's
booth. "Follow me," Jesus
told him, and Levi got up
and followed him.

– Mark 2:14

The Main Idea

The second stage of launching a Q Place is Invitation—the process
of casting confident and compelling invitations to spiritually curious
people to join a small group to discuss God and the Bible.

Understand It

Consider how compelling Jesus' simple invitation must have been to
Levi. When Jesus encountered Levi in his own setting, He greeted
him favorably while most Jews would have shunned him. Levi was
employed by the Romans as a tax collector. Tax collectors were
despised by their fellow Jews because they were considered traitors
and they often extorted money as well. Most Jews didn't even look at

tax collectors. But Jesus noticed Levi and then invited him to join His group and follow.

There was a lot at stake for Levi in accepting Jesus' invitation to follow Him, for there would be little chance to return to his occupation. Tax collecting jobs, for the indiscriminate Jew, were greatly sought after as a sure way to get rich quickly. When Levi said yes to following Jesus, he was saying goodbye to a good source of income.

Because of this invitation, Jesus and His followers ended up at Levi's house later that same day, not only with Levi at the dinner table, but also with other tax collectors and people who were considered "sinners." Levi had invited his friends. Imagine the conversation that occurred at dinner. Surely there was great diversity of opinion about God, the Law of Moses, and who this Jesus was!

This whole story fits so well with Jesus' own mission statement: ***"It is not the healthy who need a doctor, but the sick. I have not come to call the righteous, but sinners"*** (Mark 2:17). People had been labeled "sinners" by self-righteous religious leaders who didn't recognize their own need. Jesus came in a different way. Instead of labeling people, Jesus befriended them; His actions led religious leaders to see Him as a "friend of sinners" (Matthew 11:19).

In following Jesus, we will also seek to spend time with people who may feel distant from religious communities, but who are spiritually open and willing to explore what they believe about God. As we extend a heartfelt welcome, they are likely to accept our invitation to come to a Q Place.

Invitation best practices

When you are assembling a list of people to invite, resist the temptation to judge who will be interested. Let God help you select the potential attendees through prayer and quiet listening to Him. You might be surprised at who ends up accepting your invitation and attending that first gathering.

While you pray, think about the individuals you will invite, and ask God what aspect of a Trial Meeting would spark their interest. Begin praying for an opening to bring up the topic with them in conversation, even before you have worked out all the details of the Trial Meeting. If your description resonates with their individual needs, they will be more compelled to consider coming. At some level each person will likely have a spiritual hunger to know God, even if it has been dormant for a long time or never fully identified. Finding and tapping into that hunger is crucial.

As you talk with people you know about the idea of a discussion group about God and the Bible, you may bring up some or all of these points:

1. The purpose of the group is to discuss questions about God. People are respected as thinking adults and not judged. No previous knowledge about God or the Bible is necessary.

2. This group is for people who would like to discover for themselves what is true about God as revealed in the Bible.

3. This group is not for experts. It's for new discoveries. If someone thinks that they are an expert, they are encouraged to listen and ask questions so that everyone can discover answers for themselves. Everyone is a learner.

4. The format is informal discussion, not lecture. Q Place discussion guides will provide questions for the discussion.

5. People are encouraged to share their ideas honestly and openly.

6. People learn as they express their discoveries. One person's insights sharpen another's understanding as the group discusses a topic together. The focus is not on the leader, but on the questions (and possibly the Bible passage) being discussed.

7. It is helpful for the group to consist of people from different backgrounds who are willing to share their perspectives as the group learns together from each person.

8. Most groups meet weekly for about an hour and a half. Some groups meet for a shorter time if there is a time limitation, such as a lunch hour at work, or if there are childcare constraints.

9. After the initial Trial Meeting, a group will typically meet for six to eight weeks. The group itself will decide on the topic they are most interested in discussing. When the group has completed a six- to eight-week session, they can decide whether to continue beyond that period.

As you begin to set plans for your Trial Meeting and you prepare to extend specific invitations, pray together for every person you have in mind. Work together on your invitation wording to be sure that you are consistent in what you are inviting people to come and try, and be sure to make it clear that they are coming to experience a discussion group on spiritual topics about life, God, and the Bible.

Decide together how you will make the invitations—in person, over the phone, by email, or by letter, and encourage each other as you carry out your plans. You may develop a printed invitation card with the date, time, and place of the Trial Meeting. In any form of invitation, be sure to let the person you're inviting know that there is no long-term commitment required. You could say, "Just come one time and check it out. If you like it, you are free to come again." At QPlace.com there are many helpful tips, ideas, and invitation examples available to members.

Always follow up with those you have invited and ask if they will be able to make it. Then, just before the Trial Meeting, call, text, or send an email to everyone who has shown interest, to confirm the plans, provide more details, and let them know that you're looking forward to it.

Overcoming fears and obstacles as you invite

The people you invite will have some fears or concerns about coming to a group like this. It's important that you understand these concerns ahead of time so you can be empathetic as you extend an invitation. The best invitations will be made in person, face-to-face. This way you can see how the person is responding and address any apprehensions. Typically people are afraid of these things:

- Exposing their ignorance.
- Being judged.
- Being rejected.
- Being stuck in a long-term commitment.
- Not knowing what to expect.

If you have built a trusting relationship with those you are inviting, some of these fears will be minimized or could be discussed openly as you invite them. Ask open-ended questions to find out more about any concerns they express. Listen well to what they share and address those fears with short but clear answers. Read back over the list on page 41 for the aspects of a Q Place that you can emphasize in responding to their specific fears.

While the people you invite will have fears about coming, it is also important to acknowledge and address fears you have in starting a group like this and inviting people to come.

One of the most common fears is the feeling of rejection if people decline your invitation. You might also fear that your invitation will change your relationship—that the person you are inviting will think that you are a religious fanatic or interested in them as an evangelistic project. You can dispel both of these fears when you realize that a "no" response provides you an opportunity to continue the relationship as it was before, to reveal that you really do care about them personally. Then they are more likely to become open to coming in the future. Trust God for the timing; when circumstances change, these same friends will be ready. You may be one invitation away from their saying yes the next time. Patience (remember that wonderful fruit of God's Holy Spirit?) is very important in this process.

Relying on the Spirit of God is essential to dispel fear in the whole process of starting a Q Place. In John 16:13-15, Jesus gives this promise to His disciples:

> *But when he, the Spirit of truth, comes, he will guide you into all the truth. He will not speak on his own; he will speak only what he hears, and he will tell you what is yet to come. He will glorify me because it is from me that he will receive what he will make known to you. All that belongs to the Father is mine. That is why I said the Spirit will receive from me what he will make known to you.*

One of Q Place's four core values is "Spirit," that God's Spirit will guide those who are spiritually open. This core value impacts a Q Place in at least two profound ways.

First, the Holy Spirit is actively pursuing and working in the lives of those not-yet-Christians who will come to the group. God is going before you in each invitation, preparing minds and softening hearts. In fact, Jesus pointed out that no one can come to Him **unless the Father draws them** (John 6:44). In your group, as individuals yield to His work in them, He will continue to guide them.

Second, the Spirit is present with and at work in you, the initiators who will facilitate the group. Since you are children of God and followers of Jesus, the Spirit of God is dwelling in you. Trust that the Spirit is there with you on the journey and learn to hear the Spirit's voice. Following God's lead as you extend invitations is a great preparation for discussions in the group itself.

In Jesus' ministry, He listened to His Father's voice and adjusted His plans as He met people along the way. In the Book of Acts we continue to see the early church in action, directed by the Spirit. For example, in Acts 8:26-40, Philip was led by the Holy Spirit to engage in conversation with an Ethiopian eunuch. That discussion led to sharing the good news about Jesus and a decision to be baptized.

As you are inviting your friends, neighbors, or co-workers to your Q Place, be tuned in to the Spirit of God and be willing to be directed by Him. Be in prayer before, during, and after you extend the invitations. As you are following God's lead, He will guide you to those who are spiritually open, and He will work in their hearts. Bringing people to Jesus is His work!

Mary's Story

Around the time when we were praying about starting a small group for spiritual seekers, the ex-Beatle George Harrison died. In several articles he was quoted as saying regularly to his friends, "Everything else can wait, but the search for God can't wait." Here was a secular icon of our American culture reminding us that searching for God is important and should be a priority in our lives before it's too late.

We sent a letter to thirty of our friends with this beloved musician's quote and a proposal to come to my house on February 26th to check out the possibility of participating in a spiritual discussion group, a nonthreatening place to discuss questions about God. We suggested using the book *How Does Anyone Know God Exists?* written by Garry Poole. It is one of seven books in the Tough Questions discussion guide series.

In retrospect, I would have asked each person face-to-face, rather than through a letter. However, that required more courage than I had at that moment. But I did follow up with those we invited and talked with them either by phone or in person as I saw them around town. In the weeks that led up to our first gathering, I kept on praying for each person on my invitation list.

It seemed like God naturally orchestrated some encounters with the women on my list, which gave me a chance to chat with them about my invitation. For example, I went to the store to pick up some photographs I had ordered. It turned out that they weren't ready, but as I was walking toward the exit, I saw Sylvia. She said she had received my invitation but wasn't sure she was interested. She wanted to know more details. I sensed God's presence in the conversation as I explained more about our plans, mentioning many of the points presented in this chapter. When we parted, she said she'd definitely come to the first meeting and check it out. And she did. Four years later, Sylvia ended up facilitating her own Tough Questions group!

Discuss It

1. *Icebreaker question:* Describe what it feels like to receive an invitation from someone you like.

2. Why do you think Levi accepted the invitation by Jesus to follow Him?

3. What do you think are the greatest fears of those you plan to invite to a Q Place?

   How could you effectively address those fears as you invite them to come?

4. Why is it important to stress the option of "trying it once" when extending the invitation to a Q Place?

5. Which of the nine points listed on page 41 do you think are most important to share with those you invite? Why?

6. Why can a face-to-face invitation be more effective than an invitation by mail, e-mail, or telephone?

7. How do you think you will invite people to the Trial Meeting? Role play your ideas.

8. What are your greatest fears in inviting someone to a Q Place? What can you do to address your greatest fears?

9. Have you ever had an experience of being led by the Spirit of God? Describe when and how the Holy Spirit led you.

10. How can you and your co-initiators learn to practice hearing the Holy Spirit's voice as you prepare to lead your Q Place?

Next Steps

1. This week talk to at least one person about the idea of a group for discussions about God.

2. For more examples of the work and leading of the Holy Spirit, read Acts 2:1-12; 10:9-23; 13:1-3; 20:23-24; and 21:10-11.

3. Set a date, time, and location for your Q Place Trial Meeting (even if it's several months away).

4. Read Chapter 4 and be prepared to participate in the next group discussion.

5. Check out invitation samples available to Qplus members at QPlace.com. (Type "invitation" into the search bar.)

6. When you grow in listening and asking great questions, you will be able to extend invitations that are more likely to hit home. Read, discuss, and practice these modules of *The 9 Arts of Spiritual Conversations:*

   - *3.1 The Art of Listening: Why Listen?*
   - *4.1 The Art of Asking Questions: Why Ask Questions?*

Chapter 4

TRIAL MEETING

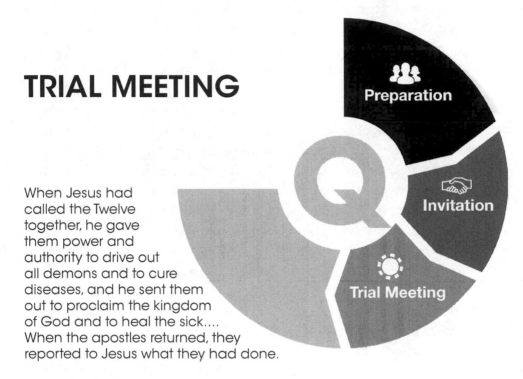

When Jesus had called the Twelve together, he gave them power and authority to drive out all demons and to cure diseases, and he sent them out to proclaim the kingdom of God and to heal the sick.... When the apostles returned, they reported to Jesus what they had done.

– Luke 9:1-2, 10

The Main Idea

The goal of the Trial Meeting is to give participants a good sample of what to expect in future meetings—the experience of a nonthreatening place for ongoing spiritual discussions.

Understand It

Imagine how the twelve disciples felt when Jesus gave them power and authority and then sent them out to give people the message of the kingdom of God. They may have been filled with excitement in anticipation of the unknown adventure ahead of them. Yet they may also have been bewildered at Jesus' command—to go to village after village without bringing any food, money, a traveler's bag, a walking stick, or an extra coat. That seems risky. Jesus gave a similar set of instructions to a group of seventy-two followers in Luke 10:1-20. He didn't even want them to greet anyone on the road! He also told this group that they should anticipate difficulties in the journey. He warned them, *"Go! I am sending you out like lambs among wolves."*

Typically, we work hard to decrease our vulnerability rather than to increase it. However, the less vulnerable we are, the less dependent we are on God. Perhaps Jesus placed limitations on what the disciples could take with them in order to increase their vulnerability. This way they would be completely dependent on God and not on themselves or on what they brought with them. Jesus also wanted them to focus on their task and not get distracted. They needed to be single-minded, even to the extent of not becoming involved in time-consuming greetings that would cause them to delay or miss their purpose in going out.

What was their purpose? Jesus had instructed them to go to every city and place where He was planning to visit. They were the "advance team." The passages in Luke 9 and 10 give us examples of the foundational plan that Jesus had for His followers: to go out in full dependence on God and prepare people to receive Him.

As the date and time of your Q Place Trial Meeting approaches, you are likely to experience excitement mixed with feelings of vulnerability. You have prepared and invited. Jesus wants to send you out with His power and authority, much like He sent out His first disciples. Until you try out the first meeting along with the participants that you invite, you (and they) may not experience the power and authority of Jesus in action. It's important to stay focused on the task, expect challenges that will point you to God, rely on the power and authority that He gives you, and remain totally dependent on Him both for protection and for results.

In this chapter, preparation for the Trial Meeting is divided into two main components: logistics and the meeting format.

Trial Meeting logistics

1. **Choose the location of your first meeting carefully.** Select a place that is easy to find and close to the majority of the participants. The closer the meeting place is to them, the more likely they are to come. One of the co-initiators might be a good host for the Trial Meeting. But if your group includes neighbors, consider the option of meeting in the home of someone you have invited who is already enthusiastic about this group.

2. **Plan for each of the initiators to take part in facilitating the Trial Meeting.** Sharing the responsibilities will allow all of you to be more relaxed and focused, and will also set a healthy precedent of group ownership. Later you can encourage the participants to take turns hosting and asking the discussion questions. This will allow everyone to get to know each other better, affirm that the group belongs to all the participants, and encourage dynamic discussions.

3. **Make the place conducive to conversation.** Minimize distractions such as a ringing phone, background noise, or people and pets wandering in and out. Arrange chairs so that each person can easily see and hear the others in the group. Also, ask everyone to turn off cell phones before you start.

4. **Have refreshments.** Beverages and a simple snack can be good companions for discussion. Make them available before, during, and even after the discussion if people have time to stay and talk.

5. **Get there early to prepare and pray.** Arrive earlier than the participants to prepare for your gathering as well as to pray with your co-initiators. Typically, you would not pray aloud during the body of this first meeting. In later meetings you can introduce prayer in a way that the participants will appreciate.

6. **Provide sample discussion materials.** Consider ahead of time with your co-initiators what topics your group would most likely be willing to discuss in future meetings. The Q Place website store and Resources section will provide many options

for you to evaluate. If appropriate, you can bring and show a few materials that you think will be most appealing to the group.

7. **Begin and end on time.** When you invite potential participants, tell them when it will start and end. Then begin and end on time. The ideal length of the first meeting is an hour and 15 minutes or an hour and a half. Make sure to allow 60 minutes for the actual discussion time.

8. **Aim for the ideal group size.** The size of the group will vary from a few participants to a large number like twelve or more, but a group of six to ten is ideal for group discussion. If a group is too large, there is danger that some of the participants will dominate and that quieter people won't talk at all. If it's too small, there may not be enough diversity of opinion for a stimulating discussion.

9. **Consider options for childcare.** When participants in your group are parents of young children, childcare for the Trial Meeting may be important. If at all possible, children should be cared for in another home to avoid distractions. Also, be prepared to offer a few childcare options as you discuss possible logistics for meeting again. While your group may rotate meeting places, it usually works out better for the children to be in the same location each week. If the group can't find a sitter, parents may take turns caring for the children. Missing the group every sixth time to take a turn with childcare is better than not being able to come at all. (For more ideas, check out the resource "Childcare" at QPlace.com.)

10. **Warmly greet people when they arrive.** A warm welcome at the door or in the meeting room will affirm each person's decision to come despite possible fears or apprehensions.

If you have carefully worked out the logistics of this meeting and intentionally prepared your own heart as well, you are ready to embark on an adventure! In the book *Seeker Small Groups*, Garry Poole calls it the "all-important first meeting." Here's what he says:

You've established high levels of trust with your seeking friends, you've extended invitations, and people have agreed to try out the group at least once. Everything is set. Now, what in the world will you do in the first meeting? Whatever you decide, let one thing be clear: if you invited people to come and check out your group without any obligation to ever come back, you'd better make sure their very first experience is a good one![2]

Q Place has adopted Garry's solid, time-tested format[3] below, and we are grateful for this contribution to our ministry. A concise version of this format is also available three per sheet at QPlace.com. (Type "Trial Meeting Format" into the searchbar.)

Trial Meeting format

Welcome (1 minute)
In your own words and style, welcome everyone. Thank them for coming. Tell them how long it will last and what time you'll end. Explain Q Place and your role as initiators. (For example: "Q Place is a place where we can discuss important spiritual questions, and our role is not to give answers, but to help all of us come to conclusions based on careful thinking.")

Introductions (10 minutes)
If participants don't know each other, name tags are a courtesy. Have everyone introduce themselves, sharing their name, where they live, their occupation, and their favorite hobby. Begin the process by introducing yourself, modeling how much time it should take for each person. Keep it about a minute in length. If someone in the group responds with a common point of interest, encourage dialogue among the participants to connect people to one another. But also try to keep the group on track.

Facilitate a Few Icebreaker Questions (15-20 minutes)
Icebreaker questions give people a chance to open up and share informally yet intentionally about themselves. Go first, modeling how much time to take and giving everyone time to think.

Icebreaker examples:

- *Where are you from and what did living there teach you about life?*
- *What was the best time of your life? Why?*
- *What is one of your happiest childhood memories?*
- *What was the best gift you ever gave? ...received?*
- *If you could relive one vacation, which would it be? Why?*

For a long list of icebreaker questions, log in at QPlace.com and in the search bar, type in "Icebreaker Questions." Click on the resource to open the full post. Scroll down to find the PDF that you may print for use in your group.

Alternatively, you can introduce *The Complete Book of Questions*[4] by Garry Poole as a way to get to know one another through great questions. This outstanding resource has 1,001 open-ended questions, segmented by hundreds, to incrementally deepen your understanding of each other and your beliefs. For example, the first set of one hundred is called "Light and Easy," while the last set is called "Extreme Spiritual Matters." Ask who would be willing to pick a number from one of the first sections during this first meeting. Read the corresponding question from the book. After that person answers the question, pass him or her the book to read a question for the next volunteer who calls out a number. Continue until all participants have had a chance to answer an icebreaker question.

Feel free to follow a different plan that feels more appropriate for your group, but passing the book and having participants read questions for each other will begin to set the tone for a shared leadership group process.

After people start to open up, you might also ask a transitional icebreaker: **"What was your faith background growing up?"** This is a simple question, but it might tell you a lot about what they believe about God. Keep it simple and encourage them to be brief.

Ask the Main Question (15-20 minutes)

Let the group know that you'd like to switch gears. Give everyone permission to answer the next question in random order, even if the icebreaker questions ended up going around the circle. Let them know that they don't have to answer if they are uncomfortable. Also, ask permission to write down answers for this question, and explain that their answers will be important in deciding what kind of discussions would work well for the group. Here is the question: **"If you could ask God one question, and you knew He would answer, what would you ask Him?"** Affirm people as they share answers, asking, **"Why did you pick that question?"** You'll often find that people share questions rooted in their personal background and experience, and that people often tend to ask questions related to suffering in the world.

Read and Discuss (5 minutes)

Now explain that before you end, you'd like to read a short passage from the Bible and hear their reaction to it and their thoughts on what it might mean. Select verses that would be appropriate for your participants, and not too difficult to understand. Two good options are Proverbs 4:5-7 and Matthew 7:7-8. Read the verses a few times and then ask for their response. Ask them to suspend their judgment about the Bible's reliability for this exercise, if that is an issue for them. The purpose of this exercise is to give them a brief sample of what it might be like to discuss the Bible together.

Wrap Up and Conclude (10 minutes)

1. *Affirm the group's participation.* Ask what impressed or surprised them about their time together. Explain that they have just sampled a Q Place discussion about life, God, and the Bible.

2. *Suggest meeting again.* Communicate that you were intrigued by their questions, and if they like the idea, you could look for resources that would help you have meaningful discussions about some of the questions that they raised, and you will let them know what you find out.

3. *Ask who is interested.* Explain that those who are interested could meet together for six weeks and then evaluate if this kind of discussion is helpful for them. Ask if they have friends who also might be interested.

4. *Share contact information.*

5. *Discuss details.* Ask what day, time, and location would work well for those who would like to try this. If appropriate for your group, note that you could take turns meeting in different homes so that everyone can get to know each other better.

As participants are leaving, be sure to thank each one for coming. If the group decided for some reason not to meet again, suggest instead a social event like a dinner or a potluck sometime in the next six months to reconnect as a group. Don't be discouraged! People might not have been ready for a discussion group beyond one meeting. There is still growth that occurred through this process. As you talk with individuals, consider asking why they aren't able to continue. You may find that the obstacle can be easily resolved.

If the group has decided to meet again and you have followed the format above, then you are prepared to officially launch your Q Place. Among your co-initiators, decide who will contact each participant who came to let them know what you're thinking about discussing if they would like to get together again. Commit to holding each participant in prayer as you carry out your plan! The next chapter will provide instructions on how to proceed after the Trial Meeting.

Mary's Story

I was not sure what to expect when the morning of February 26th arrived. Although we invited thirty women, only seven or eight had confirmed that they would come. I was uncertain about the rest. So I made enough coffee for twenty-five. Judy and Kristin arrived about thirty minutes early to pray. We prayed that God would bring those people He wanted there and protect them from any distraction that would prevent them from coming. We also prayed that God would give us courage. This felt scary. We were changing the dynamics of our friendships with those who were coming. What if they thought we were weird or religious fanatics?

Ten minutes after the starting time, my house was buzzing with a dozen women who were enjoying the coffee and pastries. It felt natural! Two more showed up as we were encouraging them to sit down in my family room. The room was full! It was time for me to say something. I thanked them for coming and affirmed them for their bravery in checking out the possibility of a spiritual discussion group. Then I told them that we were a little nervous too. We were afraid that they would think we had all the answers, and we didn't. But we thought it was important for people to figure out what they believed about God and we wanted to create an environment that would facilitate that process.

I told them that the purpose of this first meeting was to get to know one another and to find out if there was enough interest to start a discussion group about God. Then we asked several icebreaker questions that enabled everyone to talk. As they opened up, it was fascinating to hear a bit about each person's story. Many even shared their religious background and current beliefs. Some said they had no religious background. Others had been raised with a particular faith, but when they grew up they had abandoned it.

Most of those who came were interested in the question "How does anyone know God exists?" And they were willing to join us for six weeks to discuss it! We figured out a regular time and date to meet. Each person gave me money to buy the Tough Questions discussion guides, and we were off and running! I thanked them for coming, and surprisingly, they thanked me for inviting them. Many of them said that they had been looking for something like this for a long time. When the last person left, Judy, Kristin, and I praised God that He had given us the courage to start and people to join us in this life-changing adventure.

Discuss It

1. *Icebreaker:* What is one of your happiest childhood memories?

2. Share what happened in the group as a result of discussing the icebreaker question. What surprised you?

3. Why do you think Jesus was so specific in His instructions to His disciples when He sent them out?

4. Which logistics of the Trial Meeting concern you most? Why?

5. Think of the individuals who might come to your Trial Meeting. How would you welcome them, explain Q Place, and describe your role as an initiator?

6. If you could ask God one question and you knew God would answer you, what would you ask Him? Why would you ask that particular question?

7. Using Proverbs 4:4-6 or Matthew 7:7-8, practice the Trial Meeting section called "Read and Discuss." How do you think those you are planning to invite would respond? Which is likely to be a better choice for the people you are thinking of inviting?

8. Think of the people you have in mind to invite to a Trial Meeting. From what you know of them, are they more likely to be interested in discussing questions about life, God, or the Bible? What leads you to that conclusion?

9. On a scale of one to ten, how confident do you feel in facilitating a Trial Meeting? Circle the number below that comes closest to your answer. Why did you choose that number?

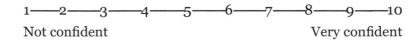

1——2——3——4——5——6——7——8——9——10
Not confident   Very confident

10. What do you still need to do or know in order to feel confident in facilitating a Q Place Trial Meeting?

Next Steps

1. This week, spend some time talking with someone whom you believe is not a Christian and ask that person, "If you could ask God one question, and you knew He would answer, what would you ask Him?"

2. As a triad or small group, watch the video "Starting a Q Place: Trial Meeting" (available through Qplus membership; type "Video Trial Meeting" into the search bar). Allow 20 minutes to view the video clip and 40 minutes to discuss your observations. What did you notice about how the facilitators interacted with the group?

3. When you are ready to plan for your own Trial Meeting, use the Trial Meeting section of the Quickstart Guide as a worksheet to cover all of the logistics. (Qplus members: type "Quickstart" into the search bar.)

4. Check out another helpful resource, "Format for a Trial Meeting," which is set up as three cards on a sheet that you may print and cut so that each initiator has a card to follow at the Trial Meeting itself.

5. Read Chapter 5 and be ready to participate at the next meeting.

6. To grow in practices that will help you facilitate great discussions—starting with the Trial Meeting—read and discuss *The Art of Facilitating 7.4: How Can We Sustain a Healthy Group?*

GROWTH: the second meeting

The word of God is alive and active. Sharper than any double-edged sword, it penetrates even to dividing soul and spirit, joints and marrow; it judges the thoughts and attitudes of the heart.

– Hebrews 4:12

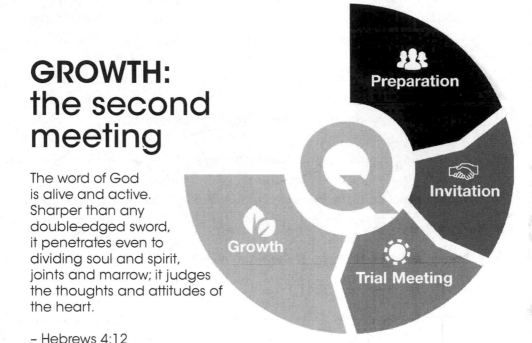

The Main Idea

The second meeting introduces participants to a new way of growing in their understanding of God. It begins a regular pattern of how you will relate to one another in a small group community and it provides a pathway toward reading the Bible and finding a relationship with Jesus.

Understand It

In 2013, Lifeway Research did a study to discover the common traits of disciples today who were maturing in their faith. They surveyed 1,000 pastors and 4,000 Protestants in the U.S. and Canada. The survey identified eight attributes of discipleship: (1) Bible engagement, (2) obeying God and denying self, (3) serving God and others, (4) sharing Christ, (5) exercising faith, (6) seeking God, (7) building relationships, and (8) being unashamed and transparent. They found that one of those attributes impacted spiritual maturity more than the rest of the attributes combined. Furthermore, that attribute was correlated with growth in the other seven. That dominant attribute was Bible engagement.

Getting people into the Bible is the best vehicle to help them reach the ultimate destination—complete transformation by coming to know Jesus. People are often ambivalent or even resistant to the Bible, but it's the best source we have to understand God's plan, purpose, and love for us. It's also the essential source for learning about Jesus' life, death, and resurrection. The Bible is the greatest love story of all time. It is the living Word of God that can expose our need for Him better than our own attempts at trying to "convert" someone. As the author of Hebrews declares in Hebrews 4:12, ***The word of God is alive and active.*** God's Word (not us) judges the thoughts and attitudes of a person's heart, and only God can open the minds of people to understand it.

One thing is clear: As you follow God's leading, and your group opens up to reading the Bible, God will use His Word to transform lives in your group. It's not by clever things you might say from your own reservoir of knowledge about Jesus. It's the living, active Word of God that will slowly penetrate even the hardest heart and achieve God's purpose. In Isaiah 55:11 God declares: ***"It will not return to me empty, but will accomplish what I desire and achieve the purpose for which I sent it."*** The prophet Isaiah compares God's Word to the effect that rain and snow have on the earth, which is to water it and make it bud and flourish.

So, as your group starts up with the second meeting, keep praying that God will stir up interest in seeking Him through the content of the Bible itself.

In the Trial Meeting, participants get a taste of reading and discussing a short section of Scripture, and you can usually gauge the interest of the participants. Many people are not sure that Scripture has something to say to them personally, and they are not convinced that it is true. Some groups just want to discuss their questions about God, and initially there isn't a lot of reference to Scripture. It's good to be careful. Rushing into something that participants are not ready to discuss is likely to reduce trust, causing them to feel that you have an agenda. As initiators, pray together and be sensitive to the readiness of group participants to look at the Bible directly. Then take Spirit-led risks to introduce Scripture into the group in a way that honors the participants' level of openness.

In this chapter, we will discuss crucial elements for cultivating a vibrant group environment, discussion options, meeting logistics for the second meeting and beyond, and the format for your discussions.

Three crucial elements of a Q Place

In Chapter 1, we asked the question "What makes this approach doable?" and we summarized the three essential elements in facilitating a Q Place: (1) time-tested guidelines, (2) trained facilitators, and (3) inductive resources. As these three elements come together in your group, you will be able to create a safe place where participants can discuss spiritual matters and explore what they believe without judgment. Let's look at these elements in more depth.

1. Time-tested guidelines. When you begin to talk about spiritual matters with a diverse group of people, they are likely to be uneasy. People relax when there are clear ground rules that will guide the discussions, maintain a safe environment, and respect each person's opinions and time.

Q Place Guidelines have been developed and time-tested by thousands of small groups. They are on our website, printed in the front of every Q Place discussion guide, on the back of every Bible Conversation

Card, and also available on a separate guidelines card so that all participants in a Q Place can have them in hand for every discussion. When initiators go through the guidelines together at the second meeting, they set the stage for everyone to understand the nature of the group and the tips for a healthy discussion. The guidelines help everyone feel from the beginning that the group will be a safe place for exploring the real questions they have about life, God, and the Bible.

One of the basic guidelines reminds everyone not to judge others. Another says not to attempt to resolve all differences. Yet another emphasizes that a Q Place is not for experts, but for new discoveries. These guidelines make it clear for all participants that they can share a belief that won't be criticized or immediately "fixed" by a well-meaning facilitator or participant. When there is acceptance and respect regardless of opinions shared, everyone can feel safe to express themselves honestly in the group discussions.

Whenever a new person joins the group, it's good to read the guidelines again with everyone. Over time, initiators can have the group self-evaluate, discuss areas for improvement, and encourage everyone to keep each other—including the initiators themselves—on track with the guidelines. See Appendix A for a full list of the Q Place Guidelines.

Checklists will also help group members evaluate their interactions as individual participants, as question-askers, and all together as a group. A variety of checklists is available at QPlace.com for Qplus members to download, print, and take into their group.

2. Trained facilitators. The definition of *facilitate* is "to make easier or less difficult" or "to help forward." A facilitator's role is to help someone learn.

There are two general approaches to learning: the telling approach and the asking approach. In the telling approach, sometimes referred to as didactic or deductive learning, one individual acts as the expert, telling listeners what he or she has learned about a selected topic. In this approach, learners are receivers of information and the teacher is the active giver of information.

In the asking, or inductive, approach, facilitators create an environment in which the participants can be discoverers. The facilitator is a guide, not a teacher or information dispenser. The focus is on the learner, not on the one with more knowledge.

Jesus was a great facilitator. He met people where they were in their needs, their understanding of God, and their own personal spiritual journey. He asked questions to help them wrestle with truth. His parables stirred up questions in them so that those who were seeking could unpack the meaning over time—probably in discussions with friends who were also there. And most significantly, He spent the majority of His time with His small group of disciples so that they could make discoveries about Him as they watched His life.

When we talk to people about God, do we meet people where they are, as Jesus did—in their brokenness and current understanding of faith? Or do we expect them to readily accept what we know about God and the Bible simply by hearing what we say?

The institutional church has relied heavily on a deductive, presentational approach to learning. Giving presentations is more efficient. Inductive learning is much more relational and messy, but it is also more transformative. As you improve in your facilitation skills, you will begin to discover the richness of questions and the importance of listening in the process of making disciples. *The 9 Arts of Spiritual Conversations* curriculum provides valuable guidance and practice to help you grow as a facilitator—especially in the modules on listening, asking questions, and facilitating.

3. Inductive curriculum. To support inductive learning, you will need great inductive resources. It may start with very simple, icebreaker-type questions that encourage people to share honest thoughts about life, and to discover that the group really will be a nonthreatening place to explore what they believe. When the group communicates specific needs or questions about God, you may suggest a topic that you could discuss together. Having a good discussion resource helps to support those discussions.

While there are many great books and DVDs out there covering spiritual topics about life and God, often the authors or teachers become the main text rather than the Bible itself. Many Bible study resources also give you an author's conclusions rather than helping you make discoveries and reach conclusions for yourself.

Inductive Bible discussion resources are filled with questions to help groups discover the meaning of a Bible passage in context. The questions move from *observation* (What are the facts?) to *interpretation* (What's the point?) to *application* (How would I put this into practice?).

Here are two helpful criteria for choosing discussion resources for your group:

1. **Is the curriculum inductive?** Does it promote self-discovery by helping you to make observations, interpret those observations based on the context, and then explore relevant applications to your life? Are there many open-ended, discussion-rich questions?

2. **Does the curriculum point participants to the Bible and to Jesus?** Even if the curriculum doesn't immediately start in the Bible, does it spark interest in exploring Scripture and the life of Jesus?

In the next section we will present our recommended inductive curriculum options for your Q Place, specifically for discussing life, God, or the Bible.

Discussion options and resources

After the Trial Meeting, have your initiator triad think through the participants' responses to "If you could ask God one question...?" and prayerfully consider which of the following options is likely to be a good fit for your group. You may present these two or three options at the end of the second meeting so that the group can make a decision together. If it's clear to your triad what would be a good fit, then let participants know the plan ahead of time and order or print the resource in time to distribute it at the second meeting. Note that many resources are available as downloads through Qplus membership at QPlace.com. All discussion guides are also available through the Q Place web store, and members receive a discount on all orders.

1. Discuss life. You could discuss a life topic that participants recognize as important to them at this time. The topic may have come into focus during the Trial Meeting or during separate conversations with participants.

The Complete Book of Questions by Garry Poole can be used not just as an icebreaker questions book, but as a book with great questions that could turn into hour-long discussions. Choose this option if you anticipate that most participants in your group are going to need a significant on-ramp to discussing the Bible directly. The questions in the 500-800 range are meatier questions about life, and are likely to stir up enough thoughts for a good discussion.

Q Place Bible Conversation Cards on real life topics work well when your group is open to seeing what the Bible says about topics that are relevant to their current stage and experience in life. Topics include Discovering My Real Identity, Anxiety, Parenting, and Where's God When I Hurt? All of the cards are available digitally through membership at QPlace.com. (Log in, click on Resources Home, and in the Resources menu panel on the left, click on Q Place Discussion Options. and then Bible Conversation Cards) Designed to be printed, cut, and shared, they include a standard format and set of questions followed by six Scripture passages that relate to a specific felt need.

The cards provide five simple questions to ask in discussing each passage:

1. What does this reveal about God?

2. What does this reveal about people?

3. What else did you learn?

4. If you believed this was true, how would you apply it in your life?

5. If you put it into practice, what could be the challenges? What could be the benefits?

Explore God (www.exploreGod.com) offers an abundance of videos as conversation starters, and a number of them work well for discussions about life. Use the questions just below each panel for group discussions.

2. Discuss God. You could discuss a question about God that the participants raised in your trial meeting when you asked, "If you could ask God one question...?" Here are a few excellent resource options:

The Complete Book of Questions by Garry Poole offers many great, open-ended questions about God to discuss. Simply choose a few questions for each session. Note that numbers 801 to 1,001 cover spiritual matters.

Explore God (www.exploreGod.com) videos set the stage for discussing a question about God. Some Explore God videos are available at QPlace.com through Qplus membership. (For all of the Explore God videos, see www.exploreGod.com.) Preview some videos and choose one to play in your group. Use the questions from the panel just below the video to guide your discussion.

The Tough Questions curriculum series, written by Garry Poole and Judson Poling, guides groups through a discovery process as they explore what they believe. It is available from Q Place either as a single volume (all seven topics with 42 sessions in one book) or as seven separate Tough Question discussion guides (one topic with six sessions in each book). Topics include How could God allow suffering and evil? Don't all religions lead to God? and Is the Bible reliable?

3. Discuss the Bible. You could read and discuss the Bible. It may start as low-key as reading a short section of Scripture printed on a sheet of paper and asking questions that will help the group discuss it. Variations include passing out copies of the printed pages for everyone to read and discuss or pulling up a section of Scripture through an app like YouVersion or through Biblegateway.com. The simple set of five questions printed on page 67 work well for many Bible passages.

When your group is ready to look at what the Bible says in more depth, check out the curriculum options below and suggest a few that are likely to be a good fit so that your group can make a decision together. Make sure that each participant has access to a Bible, or lend some if needed. It usually works well to use different translations in the group. Participants can learn and understand more as they compare the wording, so encourage everyone to bring what they have. A little orientation may be helpful. Show how to use the Table of Contents to find a book in the Bible, and help participants understand the notation for chapter and verse divisions.

Also, when you begin studying the Bible together, review the following Q Place Discussion Tips (found on the back of the Q Place Guidelines card) that will enable your Bible discussions to be more effective. Read the three guidelines, adding brief explanations (in italics) that apply particularly to studying the Bible.

1. **Stick to the topic or passage under discussion** in order to build a common frame of reference. Refer to other material only if your group has studied it together. *This will allow everyone in our group to be on a level playing field, whether we've had any experience studying the Bible before or not.*

2. **Avoid tangents.** Many ideas will surface during the discussion. If the subject is not dealt with in any detail in the chapter, do not let it occupy too much time. Discuss any peripheral topic after the study. *We can keep ourselves on track by asking, "Do we find the answer to that question here?"*

3. **When discussing the Bible, let it speak for itself.** Instead of quoting other authorities (books, church leaders, or notes in the Bible), try to discover the facts, meaning, and application of the passage together while avoiding religious jargon. *If a chapter uses terms such as "born again" or "saved," then we will be able to talk about what those terms mean, but otherwise we won't have context to understand them.*

Here are some inductive curriculum options for your Bible discussions:

Q Place Bible Conversation Cards are a great option if a study guide is likely to be intimidating. Each card has a standard format, a set of questions that work well for many sections of Scripture, and six short passages to discuss.

The following Bible Conversation Cards are great starting places: *Mark: Discover Jesus* and *Psalms: Songs of the Soul.* The cards are available to members at QPlace.com. When you have completed the six discussions printed on the card, the group can decide whether they would like to continue on through short sections of Mark or Psalms using the same format, or if they would like to try a Q Place Bible Study guide on those books. Qplus members can access Q Place Bible study guide samples so that the group can try a Q Place discussion guide session on the next section of Scripture before making a decision to purchase discussion guides. (In Resources Home, under the Q Place Discussion Options category, click on Sample Discussions.)

Q Place Bible Study guides enable groups to engage in richer discussions of the Bible when participants recognize that the Bible and the life of Jesus are worth serious examination. One Q Place participant gave this evaluation: "These study guides are great because they don't tell you what to think, but they make you think."

There are more than 35 guides in three levels. Q Place Level 1 guides cover topics and books of the Bible that work well for participants with little previous experience in the Bible. Within that level, the following guides are excellent starting points:

Mark: Discover Jesus (18 discussions) covers the Gospel of Mark—the earliest biography of Jesus. It records the eyewitness account of the Apostle Peter, one of Jesus' original twelve disciples. Because Mark's account is the shortest, simplest, and most active record of Jesus' life, we highly recommend it as the first book of the Bible to study together.

They Met Jesus (8 discussions) moves chronologically through the life of Jesus Christ with episodes from the four New Testament accounts of Jesus' life—Matthew, Mark, Luke, and John. It is suitable for groups meeting weekly, bi-weekly, or monthly.

Lenten Studies (6 discussions) is an excellent starting place for participants with a liturgical church background. It focuses on the last days of Jesus' life on earth and His resurrection.

Genesis (16 discussions) is great for Jewish or Muslim participants, and for anyone who is interested in understanding the Bible's account of the beginning of the world and the roots of civilization. It also provides a necessary foundation for understanding the framework of the entire Bible. Each discussion concludes with a Psalm that flows from the content of the chapters covered.

Conversations with Jesus (8 discussions) addresses the question, "What would it be like to have a conversation with Jesus?" It allows participants to see how Jesus interacts with individuals from a variety of backgrounds: average citizens; those who are wealthy, sick, or disabled; those snubbed as sinners; and those distraught with grief.

Remember that the group belongs to the participants and that what you study should meet their needs. You'll find that as they study Scripture, your job becomes easier. But don't rush the process of getting people into the Bible. If your group decides to go beyond the scope of resources listed above, be sure to ask this question: Does this resource help us to know God as revealed in the Bible? This will steer you clear of topics that are focused on another religion or worldview.

Meeting logistics

It's best to meet weekly if possible. The pattern of gathering on the same day and time every week helps people to protect that time in their schedule. If meeting weekly is not possible, then figure out what will work for everyone. You could start out meeting biweekly or once a month. As time goes on, people may come to value the group so much that they will want to meet more frequently.

For weekly groups with participants from the same proximity, it's great to take turns hosting the group so that responsibilities are shared, you get to know each other better, and the message is that "the group owns the group." However, if you are not getting together as often, meeting in the same location each time may eliminate confusion.

Food and beverages are a positive, welcoming ingredient, whether you have a snack and coffee or a full meal. The time of day, length of time you are meeting, and location will determine what kind of refreshments will work well.

It is ideal to allow 60-90 minutes for the full discussion (including the ramp up and wrap up), along with a 10-minute social time as people arrive. Groups of six or more will need the longer amount of discussion time. A group that meets over a lunch hour will need to pace themselves to keep within the time limits.

You and your co-initiators should plan to arrive at least 30 minutes early each week to pray and be ready for the meeting. When participants arrive, greet them warmly and allow a little time to visit so that relationships grow naturally.

Discussion format

Whether you are discussing questions about life, God, or the Bible, the format for ongoing meetings will be the same:

1. **Ramp Up** (10-20 minutes). Check in with what's going on in each other's lives or ask an icebreaker question. An icebreaker at the beginning of each session enables participants to know more about one another and builds community. The Q Place website has a list of icebreaker questions that you may print and use. (Type "Icebreakers" into the searchbar.) Alternatively, you can use *The Complete Book of Questions* and follow the same format as the Trial Meeting. Stay in the lower categories ("Light and Easy" or "Personal Profile"). You could also pick just one question that everyone could answer.

2. **Discuss Life, God, or the Bible** (30-60 minutes). In the first meeting, hand out Q Place Guidelines cards and help everyone understand how the group works by reading through the Guidelines and Discussion Tips together.

If you are going to have the group help make a decision about what you will discuss in future meetings, then present two or three options that you, as initiators, have identified, and possibly try a sample discussion of each. (In the Q Place store, every discussion guide includes a sample of the first discussion that you may print and use.)

If you have already chosen a resource, then get started, having an initiator take the role of "Question-Asker." Be sure to model simply asking the questions and having volunteers read each section of content or Scripture as the group discusses the questions. Your example will reveal that anyone in the group can take that role.

The next time you meet, have a different initiator be the Question-Asker. Be ready to ask all group members to volunteer for a turn at that role when the timing seems appropriate, depending on the resource that you are using. (Q Place Bible discussion guides are perfect for sharing the question-asking among group members within the first few weeks.)

3. Wrap Up (10-15 minutes). If the group is open to prayer, save time at the end to ask a simple question: "How can we pray for each other?" The initiators can share with the participants that they have committed to praying for everyone in the group on a regular basis. Bring a journal to each Q Place gathering to write down the requests. Periodically you can review the journal and see how God has answered prayers. This sharing of personal prayer requests and God's answers can show God's faithfulness to the participants and the love of the initiators for those in the group.

It is important that you end the discussion on time. In these first few meetings you are making an impression of what will happen on an ongoing basis. Letting the discussion extend past the promised end time will reduce the trust level of the participants. If you are not trustworthy on something as simple as when you said the session would end, then you may lose credibility about deeper issues.

Thank the participants for coming, ask who would like to host and who will be the "question asker" for the next meeting, and confirm with everyone the next date and time you will meet, as well as the plan for that meeting's discussion.

Since you suggested in the Trial Meeting that the group could try the study for six to eight weeks, plan to stop at that point to evaluate how the study is going. A good way to do this is by asking these questions:

- What do you like about this group?
- What would you change if you could?

Then ask if the group wants to continue to meet. People are generally fearful of making a long-term commitment. Give participants regular opportunities (like every six to eight weeks) to pause and decide on whether they want to continue participating in the group. But also keep the group open to any newcomers, so that the group stays vibrant and full of new and interesting perspectives.

Chapter 6 will highlight some of the important foundational considerations of facilitating a Q Place in such a way that people will grow in their understanding of God and the Bible as well as in deeper community with one another.

Mary's Story

After our Trial Meeting, most of the people came back the following week to begin discussing the *Tough Questions* book *How Does Anyone Know God Exists?* A few even brought friends! This meeting was the real test of our claim that we weren't there to give them answers, but to facilitate their discovery process. The last question was this: "Describe your reaction to people who are outspoken about their beliefs. What conditions cause you to dislike or, conversely, enjoy talking with them?"

My neighbor Marianne responded by saying she didn't like it when people were outspoken about their beliefs. That was the main reason she was uncomfortable discussing faith-related issues. She expressed hope that this group would be a place where she could safely explore topics that were "off limits" nearly everywhere else. She said what she needed most was someone to guide her and listen to her, not forcefully tell her the "right" answers. She had gotten those in the public school growing up in Denmark, where there is an official state religion. There were still so many things she didn't understand about God.

Judy, Kristin, and I were encouraged after this first discussion session. Everyone liked the material and the nonthreatening nature of our conversation. There were a few times when I was tempted to correct someone's theology when it didn't agree with mine, but I sensed that would have stifled the conversation and created barriers. However, I did have the opportunity to share my thoughts as a participant, and prayed that my life would give credibility to my answers.

Discuss It

1. *Icebreaker:* Share a time when you knew that God was using Scripture to speak directly and specifically into your life. How did you apply that Scripture, and what was the result?

2. Why do you think Jesus asked both His followers and critics so many questions when He already knew the answers?

3. When someone shares a view different from your own about a faith-related issue, how do you typically respond? Check all that apply and discuss your answers.

_____ I get defensive.

_____ I try to understand the other person's perspective before responding at all.

_____ I try to change his or her mind to match what I believe.

_____ I ask a question to get more clarification on what they believe.

_____ I walk away or change the subject.

_____ I get angry.

_____ I don't know what to say.

_____ I pray for that person and ask God to reveal His truth to him or her.

_____ Other: _____.

4. Do you agree with this statement: "Getting people into the Bible is the best vehicle to help them reach the ultimate destination—complete transformation by coming to know Jesus"?

Why, or why not?

5. Will it be difficult or easy for you to facilitate a Q Place Bible study discussion without being "an expert"? Why, or why not?

6. Which one of the Q Place Guidelines (see Appendix A) will be the most challenging for you to keep?

7. Consider the third Q Place discussion tip: "Let the Bible speak for itself." What do you think might be the benefit of this guideline for people who are new to the Bible?

8. Which of the three discussion options (life, God, and the Bible) do you think will be of most interest to those you are thinking of inviting to your potential Q Place? Why?

9. What will be the greatest challenge to you in beginning and ending on time?

10. Examine the sample Bible Conversation Card provided in Appendix C and briefly consider the five questions it asks of the passage. What do you like about this approach? What challenges do you anticipate in using it? `

Next Steps

1. Join your triad or small group in watching the video "An Ongoing Q Place Discussion." (Qplus members: At QPlace.com, type "Video Ongoing" into the search bar.) Allow 20 minutes for viewing the video clip and another 40 minutes to discuss your observations. What did you notice about how the facilitators interacted with the group? How did they respond to differences of opinion?

2. With your initiator triad or a small group, select and discuss a Bible passage from the Bible Conversation Card in Appendix C.

3. Review the list of names God has placed on your mind and heart for inviting to a Q Place. Has the list changed since you first began praying for those individuals? What do you think God wants you to do this week with what you are learning through reading this book?

4. Read Chapter 6 and be prepared to participate in the next group discussion.

5. Study, discuss, and practice the four Facilitating and four Welcoming modules of *The 9 Arts of Spiritual Conversations*.

Chapter 6

GROWTH: ongoing discussions

Then they said to the woman, "Now we believe, not just because of what you told us, but because we have heard him ourselves. Now we know that he is indeed the Savior of the world."

– John 4:42, NLT

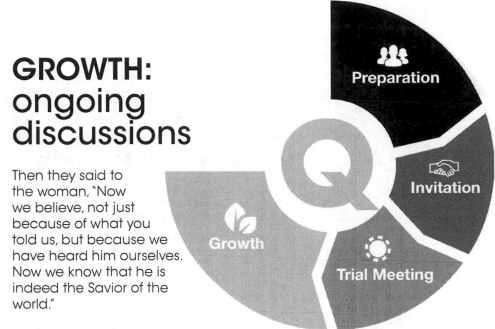

The Main Idea

As your group continues, participants will grow in their understanding of God and what they believe. You will also grow personally in your own understanding of God as you trust Him to guide you while you're guiding others. Through this process, everyone will be blessed by their relationship with God and one another.

Understand It

The Samaritan woman had met Jesus at the well. After she realized that He could be the Messiah, she ran back to the village and told everyone about Jesus. Many people from the village came to the well to see Jesus for themselves. Jesus stayed long enough for many of them to hear His message and believe. They believed Him because they encountered Jesus themselves, not because of what the woman at the well had told them.

Q Place participants have the opportunity to encounter Jesus and understand for themselves who He is, much like the Samaritan villagers did. You are like the Samaritan woman who has met Jesus and wants others to discover who He is. How can you create an environment that will enable participants to encounter Jesus? And what happens when they do?

There are seven topics in this chapter that will give you the basics of facilitating effective ongoing spiritual discussions in a Q Place. Q Place's curriculum series called *The 9 Arts of Spiritual Conversations* addresses these topics in depth, but we'll give you some highlights to consider as you facilitate nonthreatening, effective spiritual discussions. The topics include:

- Ask good questions
- Listen well
- Understand the discovery process
- Build caring community
- Remember the importance of prayer
- Serve together
- Invite people into a relationship with Jesus

Ask good questions

Historically, Christians have assumed that they need to share the gospel by telling people the answers about God, the Bible, and faith. However, people are more likely to seek the truth and learn when we ask thought-provoking questions rather than just give answers. In fact, God set the precedent Himself all through the Bible in His interactions with people. In the first recorded dialogue that God had with Adam and Eve in Genesis 3, God asked them a string of four questions: *Where are you? Who told you that you were naked? Have you eaten the fruit that I commanded you not to eat from? What is this you have done?*

We can't help but wonder why God asked questions in His interaction with Adam and Eve. He already knew the answers! God knew they were hiding because they were naked and ashamed. He knew Adam would blame Eve for the disobedient act. God knew that Eve would blame the serpent. Yet, God asked the questions. Why? Jesus asked both His followers and critics many questions too. In Mark 8 alone, He asked sixteen questions! What was their purpose?

Questions can challenge us to think, to choose, to respond with freedom. Questions can invite us into discovery and dialogue, while answers often shut down dialogue and divide us. In Mark 8, Jesus kept the dialogue alive by asking His disciples these questions: *Who do people say I am? Who do you say I am?* Jesus wanted people to discover for themselves what was true.

There's an old proverb that says: "Tell me and I'll forget, show me and I'll remember, involve me and I'll understand." Telling people something doesn't have nearly the impact as when they are involved in discovering it themselves. Powerful questions invite people to be involved. In so doing, they can also initiate community, accountability, and commitment. Often, a question is the best way to express love and respect. Questions are an essential tool of engagement in a Q Place.

So, how can we ask questions more effectively? When possible, ask open-ended questions that require more than a "yes," "no," or short answer. Great questions that encourage learning often begin with "how," "what," or "why."

Three basic questions can be helpful in almost any faith-related discussion:

1. **What do you mean by that?** (Ask this question with genuine curiosity in order to gain information about the person's knowledge of the subject matter.)

2. **What led you to that conclusion?** (Ask this question to understand the reasons for someone's belief or degree of understanding.)

3. **Can you help me understand this?** (Ask this question humbly, so that the person has the opportunity to clarify the reasons why they believe what they believe and may recognize possible weaknesses in an unsupported claim or belief.)

By using these questions strategically, you can respectfully show that you aren't in agreement with the belief without getting into a debate or giving answers before participants are ready for them. They're useful to help participants work through their own thinking. Read, discuss, and practice all four modules on Asking Questions in *The 9 Arts of Spiritual Conversations* curriculum to get better at asking questions.

Listen well

Listening is a foundational part of a Q Place. If you are effective in asking questions, listening is the essential counterpart and becomes the most consistent way to communicate that you care and want to understand. It builds trust and acceptance. You model good listening for others when you are a good listener. It is respectful. Maybe that's one reason why God gave us two ears and only one mouth: so we would be inclined to listen more than we speak!

In *Seeker Small Groups*, Garry Poole shows how effective it is to listen before trying to communicate the gospel. In fact, his book and workshops rest on the principles of empathic evangelism, which he defines as the process of guiding non-Christians to self-discover biblical truths by seeking first to understand through asking great questions and listening really well.

There have been many good articles and books written on listening. Garry references Stephen Covey's book *The Seven Habits of Highly Effective People* when he identifies five levels of listening: (1) ignoring, (2) pretending, (3) selective listening, (4) attentive listening, and (5) empathic listening. This last level of listening is described by Covey as "seeking first to understand, then to be understood."[5]

For more on listening, read, discuss, and practice the Art of Listening in *The 9 Arts of Spiritual Conversations Beyond the Basics* curriculum. It's critical that you practice your listening skills. It speaks volumes of love to those who are heard. Ask for feedback from people who will be honest with you. This is important to get right! Empathic listening will lead to great discussions. Anything less than that will slow them down.

Understand the discovery process

When you ask good questions and listen well, you can help participants in your group go through a process of discovery that impacts what they believe. In *Seeker Small Groups*, Garry Poole talks about a five-phase process of discovery that often maps a seeker's spiritual journey in formulating a new worldview on faith topics:

Phase 1: Identification *What do you believe?*

Phase 2: Clarification *Why do you believe it?*

Phase 3: Exploration *What are alternative possibilities, and what can you discover about them?*

Phase 4: Evaluation *How well does evidence support each option?*

Phase 5: Decision *What do you believe now?*[6]

While these principles are always at work in a Q Place participant's spiritual journey, the *Tough Questions* curriculum uses this discovery process with intentionality. Questions at the beginning of each of those sessions are mostly identification and clarification questions, helping people identify what they believe and why. You might be surprised by the number of people who will tell you that they've never really vocalized what they believe about many of these topics; they have never had a venue for this kind of honest sharing about faith-related beliefs.

Toward the middle of the session participants are encouraged to explore other possibilities. It is at this phase that they are invited to consider an approach that reflects a biblical worldview. Sometimes participants are asked to consider and discuss a few verses from the Bible itself.

Then as the session comes to a close, there are a few questions that help the participants evaluate and decide what they each believe as a result of the new ideas that they explored during the discussion. Notice that each phase has a purpose and a natural flow to the next phase.

If you are adventurous, you could use this five-phase process to develop your own discussion questions on a topic that is of interest to the group when there is no existing curriculum. You might also consider getting into the habit of being intentional in the types of questions you are asking others: identification, clarification, exploration, evaluation, and decision questions.

Build caring community

The most important ingredient in any Q Place is love. It is compelling. People are drawn to places where love is shown and experienced. To be loved and accepted is the universal longing of the human heart. When you invite people to belong to a small group community and give them freedom to accept or reject God, these are expressions of God's love. Asking good questions and empathic listening are ways to show love. In Paul's first letter to the Corinthians, he writes, ***Knowledge puffs up while love builds up*** (1 Cor. 8:1b). The Apostle John writes:

> *Dear friends, let us love one another, for love comes from God. Everyone who loves has been born of God and knows God. Whoever does not love does not know God, because God is love. This is how God showed his love among us: He sent his one and only Son into the world that we might live through him. This is love: not that we loved God, but that he loved us and sent his Son as an atoning sacrifice for our sins. Dear friends, since God so loved us, we also ought to love one another. No one has ever seen God; but if we love one another, God lives in us and his love is made complete in us.*

> — 1 John 4:7-12

Enabled by the power of the Holy Spirit, you are building a community that is rooted in love.

In addition to the regular Q Place meetings, there are many ways to express love and build a caring community. Here are a few ideas:

1. Periodically have lunch together in someone's home or in a restaurant.

2. Keep track of birthdays and celebrate them, or celebrate common national or Christian holidays when appropriate.

3. Have an "open chair." Encourage participants to keep the group open to others and bring friends.

4. When someone is in crisis, encourage others to support that person through meals, prayers, and practical help, such as assisting with household tasks.

5. Find service projects that you can do together to help others outside the group.

6. Meet periodically with individuals from your Q Place to get to know them better on a one-on-one basis.

For more tips on loving and welcoming people, check out the four modules on the Art of Loving and the Art of Welcoming in *The 9 Arts of Spiritual Conversations* curriculum. The four learning modules on the Art of Noticing would also be helpful to fine tune your ability to notice what God is doing all around you.

Remember the importance of prayer

Prayer is the foundational building block of any Q Place. Prayer is needed to start an ongoing spiritual discussion group, and it will continue to be a necessary component as you meet, because this is God's work. He certainly invites you to participate with Him, but as Jesus says in John 6:44-45:

> *No one can come to me unless the Father who sent me draws them and I will raise them up at the last day. It is written in the Prophets: "They will all be taught by God." Everyone who has heard the Father and learned from him comes to me.*

In the beginning of a group, prayer will not be visible to participants. It happens behind the scenes. It's important to pray before the participants arrive, after they leave, and during the days between your meetings. At some point in time, when you sense it is appropriate, let the participants know that you and your co-initiators are willing to pray for them if they would like to share prayer requests. As mentioned earlier, you could keep a prayer journal in which someone from the group writes down requests. During the wrap up of your discussion, you could ask the group if there are things about which they'd like prayer. Assure them that what they share is confidential. After prayer requests are shared, one of the initiators could briefly close in prayer, covering those requests, if your triad believes the group is ready for praying out loud.

If you're doing a Q Place Bible study, there will be another simple way to involve the group in prayer. With the exception of the Mark study guide, at the end of each Bible study discussion there is a prayer that summarizes the key points. You can ask the group if they'd like to read the prayer together as a way of closing the discussion.

At QPlace.com, there are more ideas for group prayer available in a resource called "Praying Together" as well as four learning modules on prayer in *The 9 Arts of Spiritual Conversations*.

Serve together

A special bond is formed when you pursue a common cause with someone. People who seem the least interested in discussing God and the Bible may jump at the chance to come with you to serve at a food pantry, assist in disaster relief, or join a community recycling project. Serving together invites people into a relational environment where they can belong so that they may see and feel the gospel being lived out. The shared experience also provides something worthwhile to talk about in your Q Place. It enhances your budding community.

In several scenes throughout the Gospels, Jesus asked people to participate with Him in the work He was doing, even though they did not yet understand who He was. He asked wedding servants to fill thirty-gallon pots with water when the wine had run out. He asked a Samaritan woman, in the heat of the day, to give Him a drink from a well. He told a lame man to carry his mat, a blind man to go wash clay from his eyes, and mourners to remove a stone from a cave and unwrap the dead man who came out of it.

When you welcome someone to serve with you, your experience fosters new relational dimensions, increasing common ground, activating mutual curiosity, and opening up the potential for meaningful conversations about God. There's a natural debriefing time after a service project that may organically open up into a conversation about life and God. The medium of service gives you opportunities to ask questions about the experience, share your perspective, talk about God's work in your life, and interpret the experience from your worldview. And when you spend worthwhile time together with people who may share little else in common with you, they just may catch a glimpse of Jesus.

Invite people into a relationship with Jesus

Be prepared to share the gospel message, if and when the opportunity presents itself and God prompts you to do so. Be ready, but also be sensitive to the Holy Spirit's guidance so that you know when it is appropriate to have that discussion. The Apostle Peter reminds us: ***And if someone asks about your hope as a believer, always be ready to explain it. But do this in a gentle and respectful way*** (1 Peter 3:15-16, NLT).

In addition, know your own story as it relates to your encounter and walk with Jesus. Be able to tell it simply and briefly. Be ready to answer the question, "What difference has Jesus made in your life?" We don't get numerous opportunities to tell our faith story to people God has placed in our lives. Consider it a great privilege when it happens. This is a chance to share something of tremendous value with someone else. It is a humble, genuine moment, not a time to "download" a memorized strategy on someone without discretion. If you are willing to share what God has done in your life, He will orchestrate a time and place for a conversation. Learn to listen to the prompting of the Holy Spirit to know when it's appropriate to share your faith story and the basic gospel message.

There will come a time for many participants when they are ready to hear the gospel and make a decision to follow Jesus and surrender their lives to Him. In our experience, this happens more often outside the group setting.

When someone expresses interest in wanting a personal relationship with Jesus, what do you do? When you are at the point in a relationship of explaining God's story, you have already done the hard work of building trust. You have earned the right to explain the gospel message. This is a high risk, high trust interaction. Your relational investment in the person you are about to share with makes it much more likely that your words will be warmly received.

The four learning modules on the Art of Sharing in *The 9 Arts of Spiritual Conversations* curriculum provide a great deal of guidance that will help you to become equipped to share your story and God's story, but here is a simple way to explain how to accept God's offer.

When someone is ready to receive the free gift of grace and forgiveness that God has provided through Jesus, find a quiet place where you will be able to pray together without distraction. You can explain that it's as simple as ABC:

- **A**dmit that you are a sinner.

- **B**elieve that Jesus died for your sins in your place, and that as God, He forgives you.

- **C**ommit to follow Jesus.

Encourage them to pray with you, using their own words. You might ask them to think back through what just happened and help you remember as you jot down the key thoughts and Scriptures that were part of the process for them in coming to this moment. Capturing that information in writing while it's fresh could be valuable for them to read through later, to help them remember, to begin to understand their story more fully, and to help them in sharing it with other people. In fact, it's a great idea to ask if they would be willing to share this decision with the group at some point. Then everyone else in the group will be able to see a new story of God's work in a person's life, and may also begin to consider more personal questions about Jesus for themselves. Even before the story is shared, though, that person's new outlook on life and on the Scriptures is likely to be evident to the rest of the group.

When a group member comes to know Jesus, you will see another incredible benefit of starting a Q Place: Everything is already in place and in process for that person—who has just come alive spiritually—to be fed and to grow in Him! When these things start happening in your group, pray and watch for the time when your group can multiply. One or two of your current triad could join with one or two of the new believers, and start the process all over again, going through *How to Start a Q Place* together, and inviting brand-new participants to a new Q Place.

Here is another way to multiply: Two current initiators could stay in a group with those who haven't yet come to Jesus, inviting more participants to join you, while the new believers stay together with the third initiator. That group could go through a Q Place Bible study that will ground them well in their young faith. Consider *John, Acts, Romans,* or *1 & 2 Thessalonians* (which also includes 2 & 3 John and Jude). But don't stay in the same group forever! An important element of growth is being involved in helping new people interact with the Bible and make discoveries about Jesus for themselves.

From the first moment that your group starts discussing spiritual questions about life, God, or the Bible—through the time when people discover Jesus and begin to put their trust in Him—to the time when your group is ready to multiply, launching more groups that can spread and grow—the longest stage of starting a Q Place is Stage 4: Growth. As your group meets week after week, there will be continuous learning and growth for you, for your co-initiators, and for every participant.

So there you have it—how to start a Q Place! If you have read through this book simply to understand the information before taking action, I hope that you will go back now and walk through the four stages in real life. You can return to the book many times as a reference to guide you in every part of the journey.

If you have already been putting every stage into practice as you have gone through this book, and if you have actually started a Q Place—congratulations! I'd like to encourage you to take advantage of a dynamic resource called the Initiator Forum, available through Qplus membership. It's a one-hour call running weekly throughout the year to address specific topics and to provide general support to those starting and facilitating Q Places. Each call incorporates time for questions, stories, and connecting with initiators across the country.

I hope that you are engaging with other Q Place initiators through all of the connections available through Qplus membership, and we hope that you are telling your story! As you face challenges and see victories, what happens in your group can encourage other groups. By sharing your story, you can also help other Christians catch this vision and begin to engage with people around them in ways that lead them to Jesus.

In fact, you could be the catalyst for helping many Christians to launch groups like yours. When Jesus looked out over crowds of people and His heart broke to see them confused and aimless, like sheep with no shepherd, surely He was serious when He said to His disciples, ***"What a huge harvest!...How few workers! On your knees and pray for harvest hands!"*** (Matthew 9:35-38, *The Message*). How thrilling for us all to do just that, and then to be part of the answer to that prayer!

Mary's Story

As time went on in our group, Marianne found that it really was a safe place to explore spiritual topics. She had many questions. But I knew she wasn't ready to hear my answers. She came every week. Sometimes when the group would discuss a question, I wouldn't give an answer at all. Then she would say to me, "Mary you didn't answer the question. What do you think?" When anyone in the group specifically asked me to answer a question, I sensed that they really wanted to know what I thought. I didn't have to be outspoken or forceful, because they were ready to hear what I had to say. I had tried to listen well to Marianne and the others in the group.

Marianne became our regular baker—with the most amazing Danish desserts! She would re-arrange her entire weekly schedule to make sure she could attend our group and bring treats. We often met at her house. I saw a lot of spiritual growth in Marianne through our discussions, and in time she and her husband began attending a local church.

Another woman named Denise also came every week. She was an attorney who worked part time and arranged her work schedule around our group meetings. After several months of participating in our group and discussing a few of the Tough Questions guides, Denise came up to me after one of our gatherings. In the process of answering one of the questions that session, I had the opportunity to briefly share with the group that I had a personal relationship with Jesus Christ. Another participant had also recently shared with the group that she had just made a decision to become a Christian.

These comments were on Denise's mind, and she told me that she didn't think she had a personal relationship with Jesus, though she had gone to church all of her life. She wanted God to be more personal and relevant to her life. How could she do that? I told her that it was as simple as ABC: admit that she was a sinner; believe that Jesus died for her sins as the Son of God, and commit to following Jesus. We sat down in my living room and Denise prayed to invite Jesus into her life. Five years later, after studying the Bible and growing in her faith, Denise was thinking of leading her own Tough Questions group!

Discuss It

1. *Icebreaker:* Who do you know who is a great question-asker? What makes that person good at it?

2. In your experience, when have questions helped you to make discoveries?

3. How can questions help us in talking about God?

4. Why do you think Christians assume they need to share the gospel by *telling* people the answers about God and the Bible?

5. Who is the best listener you know personally? What makes him or her a good listener?

6. How do you think you could improve your listening skills?

7. Describe a group of people (family or friends) with whom you feel loved and accepted. What do you think created that sense of love, belonging, and acceptance?

8. Describe someone you know personally whose behavior provides the strongest evidence or witness that Christianity is true.

9. What would others say about your life as evidence that Christianity is true?

10. Jesus describes "fruit" in John 4:36 (NLT) as "people brought to eternal life." Have you ever had the experience of seeing Jesus produce this kind of fruit through your own life? If so, share one example. If not, what do you think it will take to be ready?

11. What questions do you still have about starting a Q Place?

Next Steps

1. Decide where you are in the process of starting a Q Place, determine what you need, and take action!

2. Read the book *The 9 Arts of Spiritual Conversations: Walking Alongside People Who Believe Differently* by Mary Schaller and John Crilly (Tyndale, 2016).

3. If you have only read through *How to Start a Q Place,* ask two Christians to join you as an initiator triad and go back through the book together to guide you through the process of actually starting a Q Place.

4. Choose modules from Q Place's 9 Arts curriculum to learn and practice skills so that your everyday interactions with people can become more relational.

5. Start a Q Place!

Q Place Guidelines

1. The purpose of a Q Place is to discuss questions about God.

2. Initiators start a Q Place and facilitate a healthy small group process.

3. Q Place is not for experts. It's for new discoveries. If you think you are an expert, resist the urge to teach. Instead, try to listen and ask questions so that everyone can discover answers for themselves.

4. The format is informal discussion, not lecture. Q Place provides resources for the discussion.

5. If at all possible, read and think through the content and questions ahead of time. Share your ideas honestly and openly.

6. In each session a different person may ask the questions in order to encourage group ownership and dynamic discussions.

7. Maintain confidentiality, courtesy, and respect toward others, even if they don't agree with your position. Do not judge others and avoid side conversations.

8. Do not attempt to resolve all differences or conflicts of opinion. Keep moving when there seems to be an impasse.

9. Begin and end on time.

10. Review the discussion guidelines whenever there's a new person in the group.

Discussion Tips

1. Stick to the topic or passage under discussion.

2. Avoid tangents.

3. When discussing the Bible, let it speak for itself.

Mission

To mobilize Christians
to facilitate group discussions
with spiritual seekers
so they can find God
as revealed in the Bible.

Vision

Christians all over the world
inviting people into small groups
to question, discover, and grow
in their relationship with God.

Core Values

Self-Discovery

People grow and learn best
when they discover truth for themselves
through discussion and study.

Safe Place

An ideal environment for spiritual growth
is in a small group where personal dignity is valued
and leadership is shared.

Spirit

God's Spirit will guide those
who are spiritually open.

Scripture

The Bible and the life of Jesus
are worth serious examination.

TOPIC:
Fulfillment and Purpose

6 group discussions

Place
Where you come to know.

Discussion Format

Ramp Up (20 min)
Check in with what's going on in each other's lives or ask an icebreaker question.

Share what you applied or passed on to someone else from last week's discussion.

Focus on this Week's Topic (30-50 min)
Read the account, try summarizing it out loud together, and discuss these questions:

1 **What does this reveal about God?**

2 **What does this reveal about people?**

3 **What else did you learn?**

4 **If you believed this was true, how would you apply it in your life?**

5 **If you put it into practice, what could be the challenges? What could be the benefits?**

Wrap Up (10 min)
How can we pray for each other?

Week 1: What pursuits are really worthwhile?
Matthew 6:26-34

Week 2: How fulfilling is pleasure and wealth?
Ecclesiastes 2:1-11

Week 3: What brings lasting fulfillment?
Psalm 1; Psalm 19:7-11

Week 4: Why am I here?
Genesis 1:26-31

Week 5: What are the ultimate questions?
John 3:16-21

Week 6: What satisfies emotional thirst?
John 4:1-15

It started with the Great Commission

> God authorized and commanded me to commission you: Go out and train everyone you meet, far and near, in this way of life, marking them by baptism in the threefold name: Father, Son, and Holy Spirit. Then instruct them in the practice of all I have commanded you. I'll be with you as you do this, day after day after day, right up to the end of the age.
>
> – Matthew 28:18-20, *The Message*

We believe that Jesus' Great Commission was for all of His followers down through the ages—not for a select few.

But how?

This has been a perplexing question for hundreds of thousands of churches over the last two thousand years. Many Christians sincerely desire to engage in meaningful conversations about God with those who are not interested in coming to church. Very often the problem is not a lack of desire. So many Christians really do want to help people come to know Jesus, but they are not sure how to engage effectively with their family, friends, neighbors, and co-workers who believe differently than they do.

What if Christ-followers did not think that they had to have all of the answers first? What if they focused mostly on listening, loving, and discussing spiritual questions that people want to ask? What if they could be trained in several weeks' time rather than in years of a seminary education, and the result was actually a more effective way to engage people far from God?

A Q Place ministry is a powerful way to get people in your church mobilized, on mission with God, and starting a movement in your church to reach outward—and make disciples. A church that has a Q Place ministry casts vision for this approach to outreach, and then equips, empowers, and supports Christians who realize that this is something they can do.

Five phases for launching a Q Place ministry

Phase 1: Build a lead team.

Phase 2: Lay the foundation.

Phase 3: Empower initiators.

Phase 4: Support triads.

Phase 5: Sustain the ministry.

The first letter of each of the five phases spells out the word BLESS. When you start a Q Place ministry, potential initiators are blessed by what God does in their hearts and minds as they prepare to start a Q Place. Then, participants in those Q Places are blessed as they are drawn closer to God. The ultimate blessing comes when individuals actually come to know Jesus personally.

Q Place has developed resources that churches can use to integrate the 9 Arts of Spiritual Conversations into sermon series, discipleship groups, or classes as well as resources to help start and multiply Q Places. Churches can become Qplus church members and access all of the resources digitally on our website as they go through the five-phase process of launching a Q Place ministry, and we are also ready to walk alongside with coaching and encouragement.

Notes

1. Bill Donahue, *Leading Life-Changing Small Groups* (Grand Rapids, MI: Zondervan, 2002), 26-27.

2. Garry Poole, *Seeker Small Groups* (Grand Rapids, MI: Zondervan, 2003), 100-101.

3. Ibid., 102-109.

4. Garry Poole, *The Complete Book of Questions* (Grand Rapids, MI: Zondervan, 2003).

5. Stephen Covey, *The Seven Habits of Highly Effective People* (New York: Simon and Schuster, 1989), 237-238.

6. *Seeker Small Groups*, 38-41.

For a deeper understanding
of engaging in meaningful conversations
about God...

check out this valuable resource
at QPlace.com
or through your favorite
book retailer.

Resources for starting a Q Place or a Q Place ministry... at your fingertips

If you are starting a Q Place or a Q Place ministry, having immediate access to resources can make all the difference.

To support you in every stage of starting a Q Place and in every phase of launching a Q Place ministry, we have pulled together a wealth of resources that are available by becoming a member.

Join Qplus if you are starting a Q Place. Join Qplus church to launch a Q Place ministry in your church.

Just want to check it out? Simply register for Free Resources. You'll be able to open key initial resources for starting a group, and you'll be able to get a glimpse of all of the resources that come with a full membership.

See all the details and join now at QPlace.com/resources.

Features

	Free Resources ----	Qplus Member Resources $45/year	Qplus CHURCH Member Resources see pricing at QPlace .com
Roadmaps for starting a Q Place and Q Place ministry	✓	✓	✓
Web access to initial key resources	✓	✓	✓
Digital newsletters for equipping and connection	✓	✓	✓
The 9 Arts of Spiritual Conversations Beyond the Basics (36 digital curriculum modules)		✓	✓
Dozens of online resources for group challenges, checklists, and guidance for growth in your group		✓	✓
Bible Conversation Cards to print and share		✓	✓
Discounts: 20% off Q Place store purchases and event registrations		✓	✓
Videos of top-notch speakers, stories, and footage from Q Places in action		✓	✓
Phone and webinar support		✓	✓
Access to Qplus resources for anyone in your church or ministry			✓
The Qplus Church Ministry Kit			✓
The full scope of Q Place ministry resources, with customizable plans, meeting ideas, and templates			✓

Q Place Guidelines

1. The purpose of a Q Place is to discuss questions about God.

2. Initiators start a Q Place and facilitate a healthy small group process.

3. Q Place is not for experts. It's for new discoveries. If you think you are an expert, resist the urge to teach. Instead, try to listen and ask questions so that everyone can discover answers for themselves.

4. The format is informal discussion, not lecture. Q Place provides resources for the discussion.

5. If at all possible, read and think through the content and questions ahead of time. Share your ideas honestly and openly.

6. In each session a different person may ask the questions in order to encourage group ownership and dynamic discussions.

7. Maintain confidentiality, courtesy, and respect toward others, even if they don't agree with your position. Do not judge others and avoid side conversations.

8. Do not attempt to resolve all differences or conflicts of opinion. Keep moving when there seems to be an impasse.

9. Begin and end on time.

10. Review the discussion guidelines whenever there's a new person in the group.

Discussion Tips

1. Stick to the topic or passage under discussion.

2. Avoid tangents.

3. When discussing the Bible, let it speak for itself.

Mission

To mobilize Christians
to facilitate group discussions
with spiritual seekers
so they can find God
as revealed in the Bible.

Vision

Christians all over the world
inviting people into small groups
to question, discover, and grow
in their relationship with God.

Core Values

Self-Discovery

People grow and learn best
when they discover truth for themselves
through discussion and study.

Safe Place

An ideal environment for spiritual growth
is in a small group where personal dignity is valued
and leadership is shared.

Spirit

God's Spirit will guide those
who are spiritually open.

Scripture

The Bible and the life of Jesus
are worth serious examination.

TOPIC:
Fulfillment and Purpose

6 group discussions

QPlace
Where you come to know.

Discussion Format

Ramp Up (20 min)
Check in with what's going on in each other's lives or ask an icebreaker question.

Share what you applied or passed on to someone else from last week's discussion.

Focus on this Week's Topic (30-50 min)
Read the account, try summarizing it out loud together, and discuss these questions:

1 **What does this reveal about God?**

2 **What does this reveal about people?**

3 **What else did you learn?**

4 **If you believed this was true, how would you apply it in your life?**

5 **If you put it into practice, what could be the challenges? What could be the benefits?**

Wrap Up (10 min)
How can we pray for each other?

Week 1: What pursuits are really worthwhile?
Matthew 6:26-34

Week 2: How fulfilling is pleasure and wealth?
Ecclesiastes 2:1-11

Week 3: What brings lasting fulfillment?
Psalm 1; Psalm 19:7-11

Week 4: Why am I here?
Genesis 1:26-31

Week 5: What are the ultimate questions?
John 3:16-21

Week 6: What satisfies emotional thirst?
John 4:1-15

It started with the Great Commission

> God authorized and commanded me to commission you: Go out and train everyone you meet, far and near, in this way of life, marking them by baptism in the threefold name: Father, Son, and Holy Spirit. Then instruct them in the practice of all I have commanded you. I'll be with you as you do this, day after day after day, right up to the end of the age.

> – Matthew 28:18-20, *The Message*

We believe that Jesus' Great Commission was for all of His followers down through the ages—not for a select few.

But how?

This has been a perplexing question for hundreds of thousands of churches over the last two thousand years. Many Christians sincerely desire to engage in meaningful conversations about God with those who are not interested in coming to church. Very often the problem is not a lack of desire. So many Christians really do want to help people come to know Jesus, but they are not sure how to engage effectively with their family, friends, neighbors, and co-workers who believe differently than they do.

What if Christ-followers did not think that they had to have all of the answers first? What if they focused mostly on listening, loving, and discussing spiritual questions that people want to ask? What if they could be trained in several weeks' time rather than in years of a seminary education, and the result was actually a more effective way to engage people far from God?

A Q Place ministry is a powerful way to get people in your church mobilized, on mission with God, and starting a movement in your church to reach outward—and make disciples. A church that has a Q Place ministry casts vision for this approach to outreach, and then equips, empowers, and supports Christians who realize that this is something they can do.

Five phases for launching a Q Place ministry

Phase 1: Build a lead team.
Phase 2: Lay the foundation.
Phase 3: Empower initiators.
Phase 4: Support triads.
Phase 5: Sustain the ministry.

The first letter of each of the five phases spells out the word BLESS. When you start a Q Place ministry, potential initiators are blessed by what God does in their hearts and minds as they prepare to start a Q Place. Then, participants in those Q Places are blessed as they are drawn closer to God. The ultimate blessing comes when individuals actually come to know Jesus personally.

Q Place has developed resources that churches can use to integrate the 9 Arts of Spiritual Conversations into sermon series, discipleship groups, or classes as well as resources to help start and multiply Q Places. Churches can become Qplus church members and access all of the resources digitally on our website as they go through the five-phase process of launching a Q Place ministry, and we are also ready to walk alongside with coaching and encouragement.

Notes

1. Bill Donahue, *Leading Life-Changing Small Groups* (Grand Rapids, MI: Zondervan, 2002), 26-27.

2. Garry Poole, *Seeker Small Groups* (Grand Rapids, MI: Zondervan, 2003), 100-101.

3. Ibid., 102-109.

4. Garry Poole, *The Complete Book of Questions* (Grand Rapids, MI: Zondervan, 2003).

5. Stephen Covey, *The Seven Habits of Highly Effective People* (New York: Simon and Schuster, 1989), 237-238.

6. *Seeker Small Groups*, 38-41.

For a deeper understanding
of engaging in meaningful conversations
about God...

check out this valuable resource
at QPlace.com
or through your favorite
book retailer.

Resources for starting a Q Place or a Q Place ministry... at your fingertips

If you are starting a Q Place or a Q Place ministry, having immediate access to resources can make all the difference.

To support you in every stage of starting a Q Place and in every phase of launching a Q Place ministry, we have pulled together a wealth of resources that are available by becoming a member.

Join Qplus if you are starting a Q Place. Join Qplus church to launch a Q Place ministry in your church.

Just want to check it out? Simply register for Free Resources. You'll be able to open key initial resources for starting a group, and you'll be able to get a glimpse of all of the resources that come with a full membership.

See all the details and join now at QPlace.com/resources.

Features

Features	Free Resources	Qplus Member Resources	Qplus Church Member Resources
	----	$45/year	see pricing at QPlace.com
Roadmaps for starting a Q Place and Q Place ministry	✓	✓	✓
Web access to initial key resources	✓	✓	✓
Digital newsletters for equipping and connection	✓	✓	✓
The 9 Arts of Spiritual Conversations Beyond the Basics (36 digital curriculum modules)		✓	✓
Dozens of online resources for group challenges, checklists, and guidance for growth in your group		✓	✓
Bible Conversation Cards to print and share		✓	✓
Discounts: 20% off Q Place store purchases and event registrations		✓	✓
Videos of top-notch speakers, stories, and footage from Q Places in action		✓	✓
Phone and webinar support		✓	✓
Access to Qplus resources for anyone in your church or ministry			✓
The Qplus Church Ministry Kit			✓
The full scope of Q Place ministry resources, with customizable plans, meeting ideas, and templates			✓